GUIDE

HIGH SPEED

IN

PITMAN'S SHORTHAND

BY

EMILY D. SMITH, F.S.C.T.

*Holder of National Union of Teachers Certificate for
250 Words a Minute*

AND

A. J. MUNRO, F.S.C.T.

*High Speed Training Instructor at Pitmans College, London.
Editor of "Half Hours with Popular Authors,"
"Selected Extracts from Favourite Authors," etc.*

LONDON
SIR ISAAC PITMAN & SONS, LTD.
1933

2 080758 21

All rights reserved

653.42
SMITH
AND
MUNRO
copy 2

RESERVE

SIR ISAAC PITMAN & SONS, Ltd.
PITMAN HOUSE, PARKER STREET, KINGSWAY, LONDON, W.C.2
THE PITMAN PRESS, BATH
PITMAN HOUSE, BOUVERIE STREET, CARLTON, MELBOURNE
27 BECKETTS BUILDINGS, PRESIDENT STREET, JOHANNESBURG

ASSOCIATED COMPANIES
PITMAN MEDICAL PUBLISHING COMPANY, Ltd.
45 NEW OXFORD STREET, LONDON, W.C.I

PITMAN PUBLISHING CORPORATION
2 WEST 45TH STREET, NEW YORK

SIR ISAAC PITMAN & SONS (CANADA), Ltd.
(INCORPORATING THE COMMERCIAL TEXT BOOK COMPANY)
PITMAN HOUSE, 381–383 CHURCH STREET, TORONTO

MADE IN GREAT BRITAIN AT THE PITMAN PRESS, BATH
E6—(S.502)

H. 15. 3. 6.

FOREWORD

THE authors of this book have had extensive experience in shorthand writing and teaching, and in the compilation of shorthand publications. In addition, they have, in many towns throughout the country, ably demonstrated the wonderful speed possibilities of Pitman's Shorthand.

Miss E. D. Smith is the holder of the highest speed certificate granted by a Public Examining Body, namely, the National Union of Teachers, for a speed of 250 words a minute. She has also a unique record of successes in the realm of Public Examinations.

Mr. A. J. Munro was Shorthand Editor and Editor *Pitman's Office Training* and *Shorthand Teachers' Supplement*; apart from this work, he conducted for many years a special high speed class at Pitmans College, London. During that time many students trained by him were successful in gaining First Places in the United Kingdom in the Shorthand Speed Examinations of the Royal Society of Arts, the National Union of Teachers, and the London Chamber of Commerce, and in gaining certificates for speeds of 200–250 words a minute.

We can, therefore, confidently endorse the authors' views on the training of potential high speed writers. The subject has been dealt with both from the point of view of the student and of the teacher. All shorthand students, no matter what their present capabilities, will find herein much to interest them and to assist them in their quest for speed; while the young teacher will, we feel sure, read the book with equal interest, whether he is conducting a very elementary speed class—that is, the theory class—or the intermediate and more advanced high speed classes.

CONTENTS

CONTENTS

CHAPTER ONE

INTRODUCTORY

SHORTHAND has played and is playing a definite and important part in the world's progress. In political, legal, commercial, and other spheres of man's activities the shorthand writer plies his speedy pen. Much obviously depends on the accuracy of transcript, and such accuracy in turn depends to a large extent on the reliability of the shorthand system employed. That Pitman's Shorthand fulfils this condition has over and over again been conclusively proved. It is the system employed by the vast majority of shorthand writers, which in itself is convincing testimony to its merits. In the hands of an able writer the Pitman system is capable of recording the words of the fastest speakers, and it is with the desire to assist those who wish to develop their skill in this direction to the highest degree possible that this book has been prepared.

To reach a reasonably high state of efficiency in the art of shorthand writing, that is, to cultivate the ability to write shorthand at a practical speed and thereafter to render an accurate transcript of the notes if necessary, is the ambition, whether conscious or unconscious, of all who take up the study of the subject with the intention of employing it in any professional capacity.

Speed in the shorthand sense must always be a relative term. There are many, of course, who have acquired a knowledge of Pitman's Shorthand for purely personal use, and for such the necessity for anything approaching high speed is not perhaps vital, as a modest rate of speed usually adequately fulfils their requirements. Where, however, shorthand notetaking from the spoken word forms part of the everyday work of the writer it is imperative that every effort should be made to acquire and maintain sufficient facility to meet the demands likely to be made upon him, with that little reserve that can be called upon when necessity arises.

What is the speed to be aimed at? One often hears it said, sometimes by people from whom more common sense might be expected, that a speed of one hundred words a minute is sufficient for business purposes and that it is a waste of time to seek to increase that speed. Only a very slight acquaintance with the shorthand world is necessary to realize the inaccuracy of such a statement. One hears the argument also that a writer capable of carrying out the prescribed duties of the particular situation he holds can be described as efficient. There is admittedly a modicum of truth in this, but such efficiency is efficiency within a very narrow sphere. It may easily happen that a change of personnel or a transfer to another department may call for more speed writing ability than was previously necessary, with uncomfortable results. It is always advisable to have "a little in hand" in the matter of shorthand speed. In the shorthand writing profession, as in any other calling, it is those who can furnish proof of the possession of ability of a high standard who rise above the ranks of the ordinary. Exceptional ability indicates capacity to carry out tasks which are not of everyday occurrence.

A speed of about one hundred words a minute may prove satisfactory in some cases, but the majority of worth-while positions, where shorthand ability is an important qualification of the worker, demand a higher speed. And there is no reason why any one of ordinary intelligence should fail to reach a considerably higher speed, if only the subject is given the serious consideration it deserves. No one who earns, or who hopes to earn, a livelihood largely through the instrumentality of shorthand should be content with mediocrity. Let him make up his mind that if he is to be a shorthand writer he will be a *capable* shorthand writer. When what we might term a good working speed has been reached no great demand need be made on the writer's time to retain that speed.

9

All shorthand writers are not, perhaps, equipped with "200-words-a-minute" fingers and brain, but it is well within the capacity of the majority of those who take up the subject, provided that they work consistently and are prepared to give the necessary time and attention to the study, to reach a speed of, say, 160 words a minute, and it is here suggested that all writers of the system should make up their minds that that is to be their *minimum* speed.

Potential speed writing ability naturally varies with the individual, but in a great many cases students in the early stages of speed writing have too modest ideas of the speeds of which they are capable, and somewhat complacently convince themselves that those who have attained high speeds have some special quality or "knack" which they themselves do not possess. They display, in fact, a lamentable lack of faith in their own possibilities. Let such as those take themselves seriously in hand, and remind themselves that the fastest shorthand writer in the world had at one time to sit down to master the straight strokes and curves, the vowels, circles, loops and hooks, and the other fascinating "mysteries" of the art. But at the same time let them also remind themselves that first-class ability in shorthand writing, as in every other accomplishment, is not attained without personal effort and enthusiasm. It is to be feared that it is unwillingness to make this effort which is the root cause of many students failing to reach what can be termed real efficiency in their shorthand work. The *desire* to achieve something worth while is a most potent factor in success. The attitude of the writer towards his practice will influence the ultimate result more, perhaps, than he realizes. If he is attending a shorthand class he should assure himself, to his own satisfaction, that he is really seeking to derive the greatest possible benefit from the instruction and speed practice. Many students do not derive all the good they might from the hours of instruction available. Speed training must not be undertaken in a half-hearted manner. There must be determination, and there must be keen concentration at all stages of the study.

Shorthand writers well know how fatally easy it is in the course of practice to persuade themselves that the piece being dictated is just a little beyond their powers and to allow themselves to relax at the very moment when they should "get down to it." At such moments will-power must be exercised—and exercised strongly. It is of the utmost importance that shorthand writers should realize this at the outset, and make up their minds not to be beaten by a few extra words a minute. Another fact to be borne in mind is that half an hour of earnest and conscientious work and endeavour will be more productive of tangible results than two or three hours of lackadaisical "pottering."

It is hardly necessary to say that the work entailed in acquiring proficiency in the art of shorthand writing is not unpleasant. It can, as a matter of fact, be most fascinating, and there are thousands of people of all ages who will readily testify to hours of delight spent in the study and the practice of Pitman's Shorthand. It is perhaps the tendency for the majority of us to imagine that we do not like hard work, and yet it would be difficult to find any one who has not at some time or another in his career worked enthusiastically for *something* and, moreover, extracted real pleasure from the endeavour, quite irrespective of possible material gain. If the shorthand writer will but take a real interest in his own progress, not a mere passive interest, and will strive for excellence both of notes and transcript, he will soon find that his enthusiasm is increasing, and with that enthusiasm who knows what he may achieve?

The value of shorthand practice is not confined to the acquirement of the ability to record the spoken word at so many words a minute. It is a definitely educational agent. In an interesting pamphlet entitled *A Force in Education*,

Mr. J. E. McLachlan, F.I.P.S., says that "Pitman's Shorthand is not merely a system of stenography of inestimable practical value; it is a subject the study of which is productive of great cultural benefit. It is not only the best system of shorthand that the world has yet seen and enjoyed; it is a philosophical system of writing—a method based on the science of phonetics; based, that is, on *truth* so far as related to articulate sounds. And, as we cannot come into touch with truth without perceiving its beauty, it is not surprising that Pitman's Shorthand has for nearly a hundred years aroused the interest and even the enthusiasm of many thousands of devotees who have learned it, not with the object of using it professionally, but because they have found it a charming study, and one in the pursuit of which they have proceeded quickly along the pathway of self-improvement. To them it has been a strong mental tonic, a powerful agent in promoting that mental growth which results in what we call culture."

In the following pages an endeavour has been made to give a helping hand to those who are desirous of reaching what can rightly be termed high speed in shorthand. The recommendations made are the result of long experience in the writing and teaching of Pitman's Shorthand, and the writers feel sure that if the suggestions given are faithfully followed out a marked difference in style and facility will soon be apparent.

As a preliminary word of encouragement, combined with a gentle hint which the student who is in earnest will not fail to appreciate, we think we may fittingly conclude this chapter with the well-known lines of Grantland Rice—

> You wonder how they do it,
> And you look to see the knack;
> You watch the foot in action
> Or the shoulder or the back.
> But when you spot the answer
> Where the higher glamour lurks,
> You'll find with concentration,
> Mixed with much determination,
> That the most of it is *practice*
> And the rest of it is work.

CHAPTER TWO

MATERIALS

THE shorthand writer's outfit is a simple one— a good notebook and a good fountain pen. The noteworthy point in the above statement is the adjective! It is misplaced economy to purchase a "monster" notebook at a very low price if the paper is of an inferior grade, thin and absorbent, with numerous hairs on every line awaiting an opportunity to twine themselves irritatingly around the point of the hurrying pen. It is well worth a little extra expenditure to obtain a note-book the paper of which is of good quality, with a smooth, but not too smooth, surface that literally speeds the pen.

Many do not give sufficient attention to this matter and are content with anything in the shape of a notebook. A notebook is a notebook! That is an entirely wrong attitude, and unfortunately not an uncommon one. It should be obvious to any one who gives thought to the matter that good work in this art, as in every art, demands good materials. This indifference extends even to the examination room where, it might reasonably be thought, candidates would be most careful not to place any obstacle in the way of their success. Yet the shorthand examiner to the Royal Society of Arts was constrained to include in one of his reports the following statement—

"It is a great pity that the students generally do not provide themselves with better writing materials. It is no exaggeration to say that nearly, if not quite, one half of the total shorthand notes sent in are written on paper quite unsuitable for writing shorthand, full-size sheets of foolscap, sheets from letter-writing pads, scraps of paper of various colours, and even the blotting paper. One candidate attempted to take down one of the 120 words a minute tests on a couple of letter-cards, with the inevitable disastrous result."

Such criticism, surprising as it is, is based on actual experience, and is therefore worthy of especial attention. The aspiring speed student will see to it that the notebook is beyond reproach. Any one who takes a real pride in his work could not be satisfied with anything less than the best. And once the pleasure of writing with a good pen in a good notebook has been experienced it is highly improbable that the student will ever return to the use of cheap but inferior materials.

It is preferable to remain faithful to the same type of notebook, as there can be no doubt that one gets accustomed to the "feel" of a notebook which is regularly used and to the length of line to be covered, two little points that "make the difference." Experiment will show which type of notebook is the most suitable. There is a wide range available. A bulky notebook, say, over half an inch in thickness, is perhaps better avoided, as with this type writing is somewhat awkward when the hand reaches the lower part of the page. Probably the most convenient width between the lines is about three-eighths of an inch. Widely-spaced lines for some reason seem to encourage students to write in a large and very often straggling style.

A notebook which opens flat is preferable, as it is decidedly detrimental to good work to attempt to write on a page that yields to every touch of the pen. It must be admitted, however, that some writers do not seem to mind the undulating surface of the other type of notebook, but where good quality work is aimed at it will be found that the flat opening notebook gives more satisfactory service.

It may not be out of place here to refer to a point which the speed writer must not neglect, and that is the turning over of the pages of the notebook. What a scurry and rustling some people make in what should be a very simple operation! Words and even sentences are sometimes missed through a faulty turn-over. A very satisfactory method is to turn up slightly the left-hand bottom corner of the pages likely to be used.

When the left hand nears the bottom of the page it is an easy matter to grasp the turned-up corner, and at the appropriate moment flick the page quickly and *silently* over.

The pen should be of a good standard make, with a fine nib sufficiently flexible to allow of the heavy strokes being written with only a very slight additional pressure. The purchase of a fountain pen should not be a hurried or a haphazard transaction. When buying a pen the writer should not be satisfied until he has found a nib that is suitable, even though he may have to try twenty. Assistants are usually quite willing to do their best to meet the special requirements of customers. If they are not, they ought to be. A pen slightly harder than one's ideal should be chosen, as it will be found that the nib will "give" a little through use. Most nibs require to be broken in in the early stages, and final judgment should be reserved until the pen has been in fairly constant use for about a fortnight. If at the end of that time the nib is unsatisfactory for any reason a further visit to the pen depot is indicated.

Having found what is, to him, the ideal pen, the owner must realize that he owes a certain duty to his new-found friend. In the first place, it is desirable that it should be reserved entirely for shorthand. Fountain pens are sometimes used for autographing footballs, cricket bats, or tennis rackets, but if the shorthand writer has reached the pinnacle of fame that such autographing suggests he must refrain from using his shorthand nib for the purpose. Nor should the shorthand pen be lent to any one, as there is no surer way of offending the susceptibilities of a nib of class. It will almost invariably show resentment, and possibly have to be coaxed for days or weeks before it regains its former smoothness.

Another equally important point is the feeding of the pen. A fountain pen is a fastidious feeder, and demands a good quality of ink. There are several recognized and satisfactory fountain pen inks on the market. Inferior ink, or ink that has been exposed to dust, and, as a consequence, has become gritty and muddy, should never be used in a fountain pen, as the satisfactory functioning of the pen is considerably affected by the quality of the ink used.

Even with the use of good ink it is advisable to clean the pen occasionally—once or twice a month at least—so that nothing may interfere with the steady flow.

The relative merits of the pencil and the pen for shorthand work have provided the theme for much lively discussion and controversy among enthusiasts. One cannot be dogmatic on this question, but in the considered opinion of many experts the pen is infinitely better than the pencil. The work is superior, more permanent, and generally more satisfactory. Despite the obvious drawbacks of the pencil, as, for instance, the wearing away of the point and the difficulty of deciphering the notes, particularly in artificial light, there are many good writers who, from preference, remain faithful to the pencil. Where a pencil is preferred care should be taken to see that it is of good HB quality, and that it is of reasonable length, at least $4\frac{1}{2}$ inches. While the lead ought to be well sharpened, a long point should be avoided, because of the danger of its snapping in the course of writing. This possibility can to some extent be counteracted by having both ends sharpened, or by having a spare pencil lying conveniently at hand.

Some of these points may appear to the reader to be finicking, but in some things it is wise to be finicking. Only by using the best materials will the best results be obtained by the shorthand writer.

CHAPTER THREE

A GOOD FOUNDATION

It seems almost superfluous in a book of this nature to lay stress on the statement that a sound knowledge of the theory of the system is an important essential in the equipment of the aspiring high speed writer. But a lengthy experience of speed classes has shown that many students make the initial mistake of neglecting the theory and being content with a meagre acquaintance with the rules, hoping, apparently, in some easy way to become sufficiently expert to justify their making application for a post as a shorthand writer. They remain calmly indifferent when the teacher in the speed room explains various little points of theory arising in the course of the lesson. They are "speed" students and have come for speed practice, not a discussion on rules! That is a very stupid attitude and a very short-sighted one.

No one with any common sense would, for instance, consider himself to be an accomplished pianist when he had mastered one or two scales and a simple melody or two, nor consider himself to be an efficient book-keeper after having acquired an elementary knowledge of the cash book and the ledger. Unless the would-be shorthand writer knows the rules of the system and knows them well, his progress will not be very satisfactory. It is true that with a "half knowledge" of the system some people can write what they are pleased to call shorthand, and, where the matter is familiar and the speed of dictation slow, may even be able to "worry out" a more or less satisfactory transcript. That is not shorthand writing in the real sense of the word, and it is foolish to be satisfied with such a poor standard.

If those who take up the study of shorthand, with the hope, ultimately, of being paid for their services, would only apply a little cold logic to the position they would realize that it is only fair to themselves and to their employers, actual or prospective, that they should develop to the highest possible state of efficiency what is, after all, to be a very important, if not their chief, business asset. Efficiency is never a drawback, but inefficiency can often lead to mental discomfort, worry, and even unhappiness.

There is no need for any shorthand writer to remain mediocre, or worse. To anyone who is conscious of a limited knowledge of the rules of the system the remedy is obvious, and it most certainly need not be a disagreeable remedy.

The fact that shorthand is of such importance in office work that it has become practically a necessity in the equipment of anyone taking up secretarial work, may account for the indifference some students display towards the subject. It is something that *must* be acquired, and, as is so often the case with tasks that must be faced, the mind is half made up, very often before the study is begun, that the subject is a "bore." Little will be learned of any subject where that mental attitude exists. If only such students would discard their pre-conceived ideas and face the subject with an open mind, and with the determination to excel, they would quickly find that it can be one of beauty and fascination. Any one with an appreciation of the artistic must delight in the graceful and flowing forms of Pitman's Shorthand, while those who look upon the subject from a more practical point of view cannot but be impressed with the logical building up of the system, one principle following another in natural sequence until finally the complete and wonderful structure is revealed.

Such instruction books as the *Modern Course* (with its accompanying *Drill Notebooks*) and the *New Course*, each of which covers the rules of the system briefly and attractively, are admirably fitted for the purpose of revision. The revision and mastery of one chapter a day should present no difficulty to the conscientious writer, and in a very short time he will have refreshed his memory and filled in any gaps that were left in his initial study of the system. He may, of course, still possess his original textbook, and if that is so he will naturally use that.

He must not be content, however, merely to read through the rules, but should, in addition, carefully work one or more of the exercises given with each lesson in order to test his mastery of those rules.

There are many helpful subsidiary books obtainable, containing graded exercises which are admirably suited for revisionary work of this kind. The titles of a few such books, given below, may be of interest to those who feel that their knowledge of the theory requires augmenting.

> *Graded Shorthand Readings.*
>
> *Graded Literary Dictator.*
>
> *Shorthand Writing Exercises and Examination Tests.*
>
> *Graded Reading and Writing Exercises.*
>
> *Graduated Commercial Letters for Dictation.*

When one or other of these books is used, a satisfactory plan is to write the exercises based on the particular section of the textbook which has been studied, and afterwards have the matter dictated, if that is possible. Practice of this kind greatly helps to strengthen one's knowledge of the rules and their application. It is a pity that students, aware of their deficiencies, do not realize the value of such revision, or, realizing it, do not take more advantage of the facilities available.

As an alternative to the textbook we recommend that cheerful little volume *Talks with Shorthand Students*, by James Hynes. Therein the theory of the system is very fully discussed in an easy, friendly style which has charmed and assisted many thousands of writers of the system. Even to those whose knowledge of the rules is beyond reproach, *Talks* should be read for the sheer enjoyment that its pages have to offer.

It is not intended here to deal at great length with the theory of the system, but there are one or two points to which the student should give particular attention in the course of any revisionary work he may undertake.

There is, first of all, the question of the vowels. Some learners are too impatient in the matter of the omission of vowels, and feel somewhat scornful of these dots and dashes, which they suppose to be needed only in the early stages of the study. It is true that they are omitted to a great extent in fast writing. Thomas Allen Reed, possibly one of the finest reporters who ever lived, recommended all shorthand writers "to make a careful study of the vowels, and familiarize themselves with their use, before indulging in the prospect of throwing them aside as unnecessary; and when the requisite familiarity has been acquired, to omit only by degrees, never wholly or indiscriminately."

The judicious employment of the vowel signs can be of the greatest assistance in the rapid and accurate transcription of notes, and it is, incidentally, by abundant transcription that the writer will discover the extent to which vowels may be safely omitted, and acquire the habit of inserting only those vowel signs that are essential for the purpose of legibility. As a general rule, proper names, unusual words or phrases, and technical terms should be vocalized as far as possible. It is also an aid to transcription if the vowel is inserted in such short words as *apt*, *act*, and *odd*, not because the unvocalized forms could not be read, but because the insertion of the vowel ensures that the outline can be read at first glance. The outlines for such pairs of words as *amazing* and *amusing* demand the insertion of the identifying vowel in order to obviate any possibility of mistranscription. On the other hand, it is quite unnecessary to vocalize the outlines for such words as *anniversary*, *inferior*, *Wednesday*, *beneficial*, which, unvocalized, are quite distinctive.

Experience will guide the writer on the question of when it is advisable to insert vowel signs, but he must first of all make certain that he fully understands the true value of the vowels and their correct placing.

That useful little sign, the tick *the*, is not always used to such an extent as it might be. The habit should be cultivated of employing it whenever practicable, as it avoids lifting the pen and also safeguards the careless writer from confusing *the* and *a*. Points to be remembered in regard to the tick are : (*a*) it is never used initially, or when standing alone; (*b*) it is never written in any direction other than ⟋ or ⟋ .

A very important principle in the system, and one which greatly influences choice of outline, is that combinations of curves, circles, etc., running in the same direction are usually more convenient than those going in opposite directions. That is the rule, for instance, that governs the writing of a circle inside a curved stroke.

Occasionally, doubts are raised in transcribing owing to a circle or a hook being written on the wrong side of the stroke. This is especially noticeable in the early days of speed practice, when the correct writing of the circles or hooks may not have become automatic, or nearly so. A good plan for the young writer who has experienced this difficulty is to fix firmly in his mind the outlines for one or two simple words such as *space*, *bluff*, *train*, *strain*. Once these outlines can be instantly visualized there will be no difficulty

in similarly visualizing the corresponding circles
or hooks to the other straight strokes. One young
writer in a railway office, for example, had this
difficulty with the hooks, and based his writing
of them on the outline for *engine*, which naturally
was a word of frequent occurrence in his work.
He mentally "switched round" the *jn* to the
slope of the consonant to be hooked, in this way

, and his little worry was soon eradicated.

Applied to the circle *s*, using, say, the word
space, the diagram would be . With this
plan very little time is required to gain a thorough
mastery of the circles and hooks.

In the matter of the vocalization of initially
hooked forms, it should be remembered that where
a strongly sounded vowel comes between the consonants forming the double consonant the general
rule is to write the separate strokes, as in the
outlines for the words *turn* or *return*. It is only for
the sake of a more convenient outline, or for some
equally good reason, that the hooked forms are
used in this class of word. Learners are sometimes
apt to use the hooked forms on all occasions, with,
very frequently, a loss of legibility.

Another fault to note in regard to hooks is the
use of the circle *s* and the small *shun*, where
actually no *s* sound occurs. The mistake is sometimes made of writing for *impression*,

� for ⎬ *discussion*, etc., as if the words were pronounced *impres-sh'n, diskus-sh'n*, etc. It should be borne in mind that the circle *s* and the small *shun* are used only when a distinct vowel sound comes between the *s* and the *shun*, as in ⟍ *precision* (note ⟋ *oppression*), ⌒ *musician* (note ⌒ *mission*). Possibly this error may be explained by the fact that the termination is spelled with an *s*, which may suggest the circle to the mind of the writer. The spelling of the termination has *no* influence on the outline.

Vowel indication is a very important principle in the system, both from the point of view of facilitating the work of transcription and as an aid to high speed writing, and it is, therefore, essential that learners should thoroughly appreciate the rules governing the writing of the upward and downward forms of *r* and *l*—two consonants which are particularly influenced by the presence or absence of a vowel.

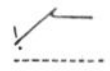

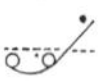

As a brief reminder to the less experienced writer we think the following two simple but important rules regarding the consonant *r*, when it is the first or last stroke in an outline, may be usefully mentioned: (*a*) when only one form of the *r* gives a satisfactory, or practical, joining, that form is used irrespective of vowels, as in ⟋ *earth*, ⟋ *oracle*, ⟋ *sincere*, ⟋ *yore*; but (*b*) when either form would give a facile joining, then the rules for vowel indication must determine which form is to be used; thus, ⌒ *rise*, ⌒ *arise*; ⌐ *store*, ⌐ *story*; ⌐ *ware*, ⌐ *wary*.

The "vowel indication" rules, therefore, must in the first place be mastered; but the student should remember that the application of this rule may be waived in order to obtain a more facile outline, as, for instance, in ⌐ *urge*, where, in spite of the preceding vowel, it is very clear that a distinct advantage from the facility point of view is gained by the use of the upward *r*. The use of upward or downward *r* medially is to a large extent a question of facility and lineality. It will be found that, with experience, the correct form of *r* will be used as a matter of course.

With regard to the writing of the stroke *l*, it should be remembered that the upward form is more commonly used.

Here again, in a considerable number of words, the form of *l* used indicates the presence or absence of an initial or a final vowel. The outlines for such words as *like*, *alike*; *long*, *along*; *vale*, *valley*, illustrate this point.

Here are a few cases in which the downward *l* is used in order to get a speedier outline: ⌐ *necessarily*, ⌐ *sincerely* (this avoids the circle and the curved stroke running in reverse directions), ⌐ *unlikely*, ⌐ *unluckily*, ⌐ *additional*, ⌐ *chiefly*.

30

In the case of medial *l* the stroke is written in derivative words as it is written in the words from which they are derived, provided a convenient outline is so obtained. This is illustrated in the outlines for the words: ⁀ *sickliness*, ⁀ *in-eligible*, ⁀ *unsaleable*, ⁀ *falsity*, ⁀ *foolish*, ⁀ *unlatch*. The effect of derivation will be noted if the outlines for *foolish* and *unlatch* are compared with the outlines for ⁀ *fallacious*, and ⁀ *analogy*. (Vowel indication has no influence on the form of *l* used medially.)

The principle of balance is another very important factor in the formation of outlines. Consider, for instance, how much easier it is to write the downward *sh* in the word ⁀ *blush*, and the upward *sh* in the words ⁀ *brush*, ⁀ *precious*. Written at speed, the outline for, say, *precious* would lose considerably in legibility if the downward form of *sh* were used. This is the same principle as that which governs the position of the *shun* hook in the outlines for such words as ⁀ *Prussian*, ⁀ *reception*, etc.

Full advantage is not always taken by students of the speed possibilities of the Halving and Doubling Principles. The Halving Principle is probably one of the most important in the system, as there are thousands of words to which it is applied. The two predominating rules governing the application of this principle are: *t* or *d* may be expressed by halving (*a*) when a consonant has a final hook or *ns* circle, or a finally joined diphthong; and (*b*) usually in words of more than one syllable.

Learners sometimes make the mistake of representing such words as *thread, fled, bright*, by the Halving Principle, forgetting that the rule (*a*) refers to consonants with *final* hooks, not initial hooks.

One or two further points which should be specially noted are—

1. In past tenses it is the *final* stroke that must be halved for the representation of *-ted or -ded*, as in, ⌄ *note*, ⊓ *noted*; —⊗ *expend*, ⌝⊗ *expended*; ⌐ *grade*, ⊓ *graded*; ⌒ *lift*, ⌒ *lifted*.

2. When the final syllables *-ted* and *-ded* are immediately preceded by *t* or *d*, they are represented by a half-length *t* or *d* disjoined; thus, ⌐ *treated*, | *dated*, ⌐ *dreaded*. A common error in beginners' work is the *over* use of the disjoined *-ted*. *It is used only after another t or d*, and it is quite wrong, therefore, to employ it in the outline for *rated* ⌒ , where the *-ted* follows *ray*. Compare the outline for the word *irritated* ⌒ with that for *rated*.

3. The use of the thickened forms ⌢ ⌣ ⌐ ⌝ is sometimes overlooked, with the result that

lengthier and more awkward outlines are employed.

4. A half-length *ray* never stands alone or with circle *s* added *finally*; as ⟋ *rate*, ⟋ *rates*, but ⌣ *merit*, ⌣ *sort*.

The Doubling Principle is a favourite with all writers to whom facility, speed, and grace appeal, and both in the formation of single outlines and phrases full use should be made of it. There is a fine feeling of satisfaction in letting a double-length stroke "go!" Some students are inclined to make too little use of the phrasing possibilities of the Doubling Principle, where there is great scope for the formation of flowing, speed-producing forms. The value of the Doubling Principle is most appositely expressed by Mr. James Hynes in *Lecturettes on Pitman's Shorthand*. He says, *inter alia*, "Knowing as I do the great utility of the principle in actual note-taking, knowing how easy it is to write and read, and how extended are the possibilities of the principle in the hands of a writer who is thoroughly master of it, I venture to express the hope that you will do all you can to make yourself a perfect master of this easily learned and readily applied principle. It has been said that the secret of all power is to save your force, and if you want high pressure you must choke off waste. There is no doubt of the truth of this, and I think the application of the Doubling Principle in Pitman's Shorthand exemplifies it. Its use unquestionably saves force and chokes off waste of energy. In the course of half an hour's note-taking the use of the principle enables the writer to save very many inflections of the hand that would otherwise be necessary and would involve a considerable expenditure of energy on the part of the note-taker."

Verb. sap.

Although we have here been able to touch but lightly on certain points of theory, we nevertheless must emphasize once more the gravity of the mistake made by many learners of imagining that a scrappy knowledge of the rules is sufficient. Few, if any, succeed in reaching the higher flights without having first laid a sure foundation by acquiring a sound knowledge of the rules of the system, which, when all is said and done, is only applied common sense.

It is, of course, not only from textbooks that one's knowledge of theory may be augmented, just as it is not purely from books on grammar that one acquires a knowledge of a language. One of the finest ways of building up an extensive vocabulary is by abundant reading practice, and it is a surprising fact that teachers of shorthand generally find it a matter of no small difficulty to impress upon the minds of some students how absolutely essential it is that they should *read* as well as write shorthand; and this in spite of the reiterated testimony of expert shorthand writers attributing a large measure of their success as high speed writers to the benefits derived from the regular practice of carefully reading well-written and printed shorthand. Shorthand reading is, indeed, so closely associated with the successful practice of the art that it should be looked upon as an essential part of the study.

Mr. W. F. Smart, holder of Pitman's Speed Certificate for 220 words a minute, says that "the systematic reading of printed shorthand is one of the short cuts to the acquisition of speed. It perfects a student's knowledge of the theory, and instinctively impresses upon the mind the correct outlines, and familiarizes him with the best phrases and contractions."

Mr. Sidney Godfrey, the famous international speed champion, and holder of Pitman's Speed Certificate for 230 words a minute, says that in high speed writing a large vocabulary is required, and that "this can be acquired by a careful reading of as many of the standard shorthand publications as possible."

Such expressions of opinion could be multiplied a thousand-fold, but these are sufficiently representative to suffice, and should encourage the earnest student to avail himself of the extensive shorthand literature which lies at his command.

It may be that to a certain type of student the very wealth of opportunity so far as reading matter is concerned may cause him to set less value upon it than did the student of earlier days, when shorthand literature was less plentiful; and, if that be the case, the loss is most certainly that of the present-day pupil.

The chief advantage of systematic shorthand reading is that it keeps before the eye of the reader the correct forms for words and phrases, which are almost unconsciously imprinted on his mind; and it is this familiarity with the outlines for an ever increasing number of words which is such an important factor in the attainment of a good speed. Further, it naturally greatly increases the facility with which the student can read his own notes.

The regular perusal of well-written notes and shorthand literature generally, quite apart from the undoubted commercial value of the practice, can be productive of a very real pleasure—a pleasure of which many students unknowingly rob themselves.

We would suggest that, when reading from a shorthand periodical, the same passage should be read a number of times, in order that the outlines and phrases may make an ineffaceable impression.

Most of us, since the days when our pocket money would "run to it," have been buying books, according to our bent, and building up, in greater or less degree, a library of which we are usually very proud and from which we derive many pleasurable hours. To shorthand writers we recommend the addition of a shorthand section to the home library. There is a wealth of short-hand reading material obtainable—*Alice in Wonderland, A Christmas Carol, The Strange Case of Dr. Jekyll and Mr. Hyde, The Return of Sherlock Holmes, Selected Extracts from Favourite Authors*, to mention but a few—and many students and writers of the system are the possessors of quite an extensive shorthand library which has been to them a source of enjoyment and profit.

Shorthand writers who acquire the *reading* habit will be amply repaid.

CHAPTER FOUR

GRAMMALOGUES AND CONTRACTIONS

SPECIAL attention *must* be given to the Grammalogues and Contractions. In many theory and even speed classes students show what can only be termed a lamentable ignorance of these most useful abbreviations, and, strangely enough, a great reluctance to make good the deficiency, even though they cannot fail to recognize the great value of these forms from a speed point of view.

One often hears students say that they cannot learn the Grammalogues and Contractions, but that is a very weak admission to make. The fact is probably that they have never made a real attempt to master them. Students of ordinary intelligence should find no difficulty in acquiring a perfect knowledge of these signs, if only they will exercise a little concentration. Let them cease from suggesting to themselves that such a task is beyond their abilities. It is nothing of the sort.

Let us here deal first of all with the Grammalogues. The distinctive feature of a logogram (the shorthand sign for a grammalogue) is that it consists of a single stroke sign, normal length, half length, or double length, with or without an initial or a final attachment. Logograms, which may or may not represent all the consonants in a grammalogue, may be grouped in the following classes—

(*a*) Those which are contracted, but written in the correct position, as ⌐ *advantage*, ⌐ *several*, ⌐ *whether*, ⌐ *thank*.

(*b*) Those of frequent occurrence written on the line, irrespective of the rule for position writing, as ⌐ *be*, | *it*, | *do*,) *was*, ⌐ *truth*.

(*c*) Those written out of their proper position in order to avoid possible clashing with some others, as ⌐ *me*, ⌐ *over*, ⌐ *much*, ⌐ *more*.

(*d*) Those which are not written in strict accordance with textbook rules, as) *therefore*, ⌐ *writer*, ⌐ *are*, ⌐ *great*.

The phonetically arranged list, which is given in the textbooks, and also issued separately (*The Grammalogues and Contractions of Pitman's Shorthand*), is perhaps the most suitable for learning, and any one who feels a little weak in his knowledge of the grammalogues should work through this list systematically. It should not take long, and the small effort involved will be adequately rewarded.

In the list in question the grammalogues are arranged in the order of the shorthand alphabet, and it is a good plan to deal with each letter separately. For instance, in the group based on the consonant *p* there are ten shorthand signs to be memorized, representing thirteen words: *put, special, specially, speak, principal, principally, principle, people, surprise, surprised, particular, opportunity, spirit*. These shorthand signs should be copied carefully on a line of the notebook, one outline for each word represented, thus—

It will be seen that where a logogram represents two words the sign is written twice. The forms should then be written on the second line, the word being repeated mentally as the sign is written. The other lines on the page should be filled up in the same way, and by the time the last line is reached the little group should have been thoroughly mastered.

Next the group under the consonant *b* can be worked through in a similar way, and so on until the whole list has been covered. The pages of the notebook containing this grammalogue "drill" should be returned to periodically, and a few minutes' practice indulged in, until the last lingering doubt in regard to grammalogues has been removed.

The Contractions, General and Special, can be treated in groups in much the same way. These can conveniently be practised in alphabetical order, taking, say, a dozen at a time.

It may not be out of place here to remind readers that General Contractions are formed by the omission of—

p in words where the *p* is only lightly sounded.

k or *g* between *ng-t* and between *ng-sh*.

t between circle *s* and a following consonant.

n in words like ⌇ *passenger*, ⌇ *emergency*, etc.

r in words like ⌇ *remonstrate*, ⌇ *demonstration*.

-ect in words like, ⌇ *expect-ed*, etc.

-kt in words like ⌇ *productive*, etc.

Derivatives are formed from contracted outlines by attaching a prefix or a suffix, as in ⌇ *respect*, ⌇ *disrespect*, ⌇ *respectively*.

Special Contractions are formed according to the following rules—

(*a*) By employing the first two or three strokes of the full outline, as in the words, ⌇ *capable*, ⌇ *perform-ed*, ⌇ *advertise-d-ment*, ⌇ *regular*, ⌇ *unanimous-ly*, *unanimity*, ⌇ *henceforth*.

(*b*) By medial omission, as in the words, ⌇ *intelligence*, ⌇ *sympathetic*, ⌇ *satisfactory*, ⌇ *falsification*.

(*c*) By the use of logograms, as in the words, ⌇ *thankful*, ⌇ *something*, ⌇ *remarkable*.

(d) By intersection, as in the words, ⨉ *enlarge,* ⨉ *nevertheless,* ⨉ *notwithstanding.*

As Grammalogues and Contractions form such a large percentage of the words in common use it is well worth while, and by no means a formidable task, for the student to undertake the systematic study of the lists, as suggested above.

It is a very interesting and profitable pastime to endeavour to compile exercises in narrative form consisting entirely of Grammalogues and Contractions, the composition to be written in shorthand. The following example will give a good idea of what is meant.

I was rather surprised when the gentleman who is largely responsible for the organization of the performance to be given in February of next year informed me that he had had great difficulty in interesting a sufficient number of people in the project, notwithstanding that all the performers are most capable and efficient. Financially, everything is very satisfactory, as several influential individuals have sent substantial subscriptions. We wish, however, to interest a larger number of the general public, and particulars of the performance are to be given regularly henceforth in all the Southern publications. This should, I think, improve our prospects.

This exercise, and any others which may be compiled on similar lines, will provide excellent material for dictation purposes, and should be practised from time to time until, as absolute familiarity with the logograms and contractions is gained, they can be written at very high speeds.

The writer who will go to the very small trouble entailed to acquire a perfect knowledge of the grammalogues and contractions has done much to smooth his path to high speed.

CHAPTER FIVE

PHRASEOGRAPHY

STUDENTS of Pitman's Shorthand nowadays are introduced to phrasing at such an early stage, and in most cases accept it as a matter of course, that it may not be easy for them to realize that in the early editions of the Pitman textbooks there was no mention of phrasing, for the simple reason that it had not been thought of. As a matter of fact, although the system was first published in 1837, it was not until some years later that the speed producing possibilities of phrasing were, up to a point, appreciated. Eight years passed before a textbook embodying the principles of phrasing was issued—the *Manual* of 1845. Even then, however, the inventor did not go very deeply into this phase of the subject, and the list of phrases given amounted to only fifty of a very simple character.

The late Thomas Allen Reed, one of the foremost of Isaac Pitman's disciples, has described, in one of his contributions to the literature of shorthand, the thrill of pleasure and amazement he experienced when his eye first lighted on the simple phrase ⁓. Although this and thousands of other phrases are more or less commonplace to the writers of to-day, to him it was a revelation, and it inspired him to further research and experiment. Soon he realized the amazing speed possibilities of this new-found principle, and gradually he compiled a list of phrases, which were embodied in a book entitled the "Phonographic Phrase Book, a General Explanation of the Principle of Phraseography; or, the writing of entire phrases without lifting the pen, as applied to Pitman's Phonetic Shorthand: with several thousand illustrations." That was in 1855, and the volume contained a note of appreciation of Mr. Reed's services in the advancement of the system from the pen of the inventor.

Subsequently Isaac Pitman himself issued an improved and enlarged "Phrase Book," which has gone through many editions, and in its present up-to-date form is recognized as the standard book on the subject.

Most students realize the speed potentialities of phrasing, but not all of them, we are afraid, have carefully and systematically studied the principles upon which it is based, and have therefore not benefited to the extent to which they might.

Those who wish to reach "reporting" speed must have a sound knowledge of the manner in which the various principles are utilized in the formation of phrases, and, in addition, should be able to apply these principles rapidly and instinctively.

A word of warning is here necessary. Phrasing must not, as it easily can, be overdone. Many students, in their enthusiasm for this fascinating phase of the subject, have a mild "mania" for phrasing on every possible occasion, with the result that instead of increasing their speed they definitely retard their progress. Phrases which may, when written slowly—perhaps in a letter to a friend or in a diary—look "pretty," are not always capable of standing the test of practical work, and it is the *practical* phrase, for use in *practical* work, which should seriously interest the high speed writer. It is, therefore, very much better in the earlier days of speed writing to confine oneself to straightforward, orthodox phrases. Later, when experience has been gained, the writer can experiment with phrases of a more advanced type. First of all, however, he should fully appreciate all the methods of phrase writing explained in the textbooks and in the *Phonographic Phrase Book*.

The chief essentials of phraseography are, first, legibility; secondly, easy joinings; and thirdly, lineality in writing, and moderate length. Even easy joinings should not be allowed to descend more than two, or occasionally three, strokes below the line.

A brief résumé of the manner in which the principles of the system lend themselves to phrasing is given below—

1. The small circle may be used to represent *as, is, has, his, us*.

2. The large initial circle for *as we, as* and *w, as* and *s*; the large medial circle for *is* and *s, his* and *s, s* and *s*; and the large final circle for *s* and *has, s* and *is*.

3. The loop *st* for *first*, the loop *nst* for *next*.

4. The *r* and *l* hooks for *our, all, only*, and a few miscellaneous words.

5. The *n* hook for *than, been, on*, and *own*.

6. The *f* or *v* hook for *have, of, off, after-, even-*, and in a few common phrases.

7. The circle *s* and *shun* hook for *association*.

8. The halving principle for *it, to, not, would, word*, and in a few common phrases.

9. The doubling principle for *there, their, other, dear*.

10. Omission of non-essential consonants.

11. Omission of the syllable *con-*, and a few other common syllables.

12. Omission of any logogram or logograms, providing the phraseogram is legible.

13. The principle of intersection.

It will be seen, therefore, that phrasing in the

main follows well-defined principles, and the keen student will find it greatly to his advantage if he makes himself master of those principles and their application. We recommend a careful study of the various sections of the introduction to the *Phonographic Phrase Book*, where these principles, very fully illustrated, are dealt with *in extenso*, followed by a list of some 2,400 everyday phrases in letterpress and shorthand, and a series of skilfully compiled exercises embodying practically all the phrase forms in the volume.

A point we would like to impress upon those who follow this advice is that they are not expected to *learn* thousands of phrases "by heart." It is the systematic acquirement of a knowledge of the *principles* of phrasing that we recommend, for if the principles are clearly understood their practical application will follow as a matter of course. For instance, if it is fully appreciated that the *n* hook may be used in phrasing for the representation of the words *been, than, own,* or *on,* such phrases as *have been, already been, recently been; more than, fewer than, better than; your own, their own, our own; carry on, carried on, carrying on, later on* should flow from the pen without hesitation.

The primary task of the writer who is really interested in phraseography is, we repeat, to become fully conversant with these principles, and, within commonsense limits, to exploit them to the fullest possible extent.

In taking notes from dictation, however, one must not become obsessed with the idea that, where a combination of words occur which are given in the official list as a "phrase," they must be joined at all costs, as this state of mind can be very detrimental to speed. For instance, we have seen students write such a phrase as *had been* with the ordinary form for been, and then, remembering that the word *been* could have been represented by the *n* hook attached to the *had*, go back, strike a wavy line through the full-length *been* and endeavour to attach the hook to the *had*. That is a bad habit, very much to be avoided. It is far better to forge ahead, and get a correct note of what is being dictated. In the notes of even the best writers one can usually see such trifling departures from the strictly orthodox forms.

Another point that might be mentioned is that some writers find that certain forms, used officially and by other writers, do not come "sweetly" from their pens, and yet they feel obliged to employ them because the outlines are used in the textbooks. If, say, a writer finds that the phrase *I think you will agree* $\sqrt{}$ is, for some reason, "awkward" from his standpoint and that he can more quickly represent the phrase thus $\langle\,\diagup$, he should by all means adopt the latter, bearing in mind that the sole purpose of phrasing is to speed, not hinder, the pen.

For gaining facility in the writing of phrases the *Phrase Drill Notebook*, mentioned on page 75, is an excellent medium.

With greater experience in the reading and writing of the system there will naturally be increased facility in the use of phrasing, and the writer may then safely "experiment" a little for himself, and give attention to what may be termed specialized phrases. It may be that in the course of his daily work he has frequently to write certain combinations of words which are peculiar to his particular profession. In such cases it is quite unnecessary that such very familiar expressions should be written fully on every occasion, and it is here that the writer can put into practice his knowledge of the fundamental rules of phrasing and adapt them to his special requirements. He is, let us suppose, employed in the motor trade, and has over and over again to write the word *automatic* in such phrases as *automatic clutch, automatic lubrication, automatic regulation, automatic valve,* and so on. It is obvious that it is a waste of time to write the word *automatic* in full, and, remembering the principle of intersection, he will arrive at the conclusion that an intersected *t* is quite sufficient to indicate *automatic* in his work.

The principle of intersection can, as a matter of fact, be extensively used for phrasing purposes in specialized matter. The stroke *p*, for instance, which is used to represent *party* in political matter, may represent *policy, period, pump*, etc., in other types of matter where these words are of frequent occurrence.

In such experiments it should always be remembered, however, that a phrase must be not only easily written, but must also be *distinctive*. As will be realized, a phrase may fulfil the first of these requirements, but may fail on the point of distinctiveness. Some phrases employed by inexperienced writers have often been quite beautiful, the only detail in which they have later been found wanting being in the matter of legibility. That, it must be admitted, is a definite weakness!

For the benefit of shorthand writers employed in specialized trades or professions there are a number of technical phrase books available. The study of the phrases in these books, which are compiled by expert shorthand writers with special experience in the particular branch of shorthand writing dealt with, will be found very helpful.

Rightly used, phrasing can be made a source of real pleasure as well as of profit. The system abounds in compact and legible phrases—phrases

which not only please the eye but serve gracefully the end for which they have been designed—
and the enthusiastic Pitmanite has at his command a medium for the pleasant, even thrilling,
exercise of enterprise and resourcefulness.

CHAPTER SIX

STYLE OF WRITING

WHEN one receives a letter with the address written in longhand, it is an almost universal habit to glance at the writing on the envelope as a guide to the identity of the sender. We all know how frequently that glance supplies us with the desired information, a proof that there is something individual, or characteristic, about the longhand writing of our correspondents. We all use the same alphabet and form the letters in more or less the same way, and yet there is something in the handwriting of each of us that "labels" it ours.

Some people write in a clear, flowing style, others write clearly, but in a stilted, laboured manner, while others again write in an almost indecipherable, or quite indecipherable, style. The few write beautifully.

Just as longhand displays individual characteristics, so also does shorthand, and an examination of the shorthand of different writers will show idiosyncrasies of style in quite as marked a degree. There will be neat, light notes, heavily written notes, untidy notes, small, packed notes, large scrawly notes, uncertain and characterless notes, and there will be notes, let us hope, whose grace and beauty will gladden our hearts—notes written by someone fully appreciative of the artistic possibilities of Pitman's Shorthand. While the purely personal touch will always remain, the system can be written gracefully by any one who cares to take the necessary trouble to acquire the habit. Apart from the aesthetic pleasure, there is a sound practical value in good notes, for, coming to the real test of all shorthand writing, well-written and accurately formed notes can be read with ease and expedition.

It is not suggested here that it is necessary or even desirable for all writers to adopt a uniform style, but there should undoubtedly be a definite attempt on the part of students, for obvious reasons, to acquire a style that is at once clear, graceful in formation, and, as a natural conse-quence, easy to read.

Too many students, through lack of thought, or maybe lack of encouragement, are indifferent to the quality of their notes, and seem to make no real effort to bring about an improvement. If only they would take a little pride in the appear-ance of their work they would extract a great deal of pleasure and satisfaction from their efforts—they would, indeed, "work for the joy of the working." The question the shorthand writer should ask himself as he looks at a page of his notes is "Would these notes serve as a model for a beginner?" If he cannot truthfully assure himself that they would, then he ought, in his own interests, to direct his closest attention to the cultivation of a style that will have some claim to being classified as good.

The copying of printed or lithographed shorthand, of which there is a generous supply available, and regular taking down of matter well below one's speed, are excellent means of eventually stamping one's notes with that little something that spells "finish," the hall-mark of the accomplished writer.

In such practice attention to detail is of the greatest importance. Care must be taken, for instance, to slope *p, b, ch, j,* and to keep *t* and *d* perpendicular, so that there may be no confusion of these strokes; to close the circles and to keep the hooks open; to show clearly the *s* inside a hook, and to form the large and small circles and hooks in unmistakable fashion. It is advisable to exaggerate the large circles, particularly the final *ses.* It is not suggested that in copying work the outlines should be "drawn": the ideal is correctness of form combined with fluency in writing.

It may not be inappropriate here to quote from the remarks of a well-known reporter He says that "the student, in his early efforts, cannot be too careful in preserving the exact shape and positions of the letters, first, because this is essential in training the hand to accuracy of form, and secondly, because he has not learned by experience where and to what extent a departure from the exact outline may be safely allowed. When he has acquired this experience, not by reading only, but by actual practice in writing, he may to some extent relax the reins with which his brain has been regulating and checking the movements of his impatient fingers, and permit them to dash forward at a pace which would have been altogether hazardous when they were ignorant of the perils of the road. The difference between a careful and a careless writer is that, while both may write rapidly and indulge in departures from orthodox forms, rounding angles, and extemporizing unauthorized abbreviations, the one knows where he may do this with safety and keeps within reasonable limits: the other puts no restraint upon his erratic tendencies, and consequently tumbles into innumerable pitfalls."

The habit of accuracy in details, once formed, will in time become "second nature," and the work of transcribing will be easy and pleasurable.

As a matter of interest a few examples of speed notes, taken from the notebooks of writers all capable of high speeds, are here reproduced. The differences in style and penmanship are obvious, but, though none of them is necessarily to be taken as a model, one and all possess the virtue of neatness and legibility.

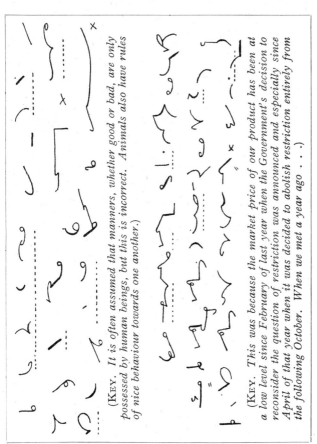

(KEY. It is often assumed that manners, whether good or bad, are only possessed by human beings, but this is incorrect. Animals also have rules of nice behaviour towards one another.)

(KEY. This was because the market price of our product has been at a low level since February of last year when the Government's decision to reconsider the question of restriction was announced and especially since April of that year when it was decided to abolish restriction entirely from the following October. When we met a year ago . . .)

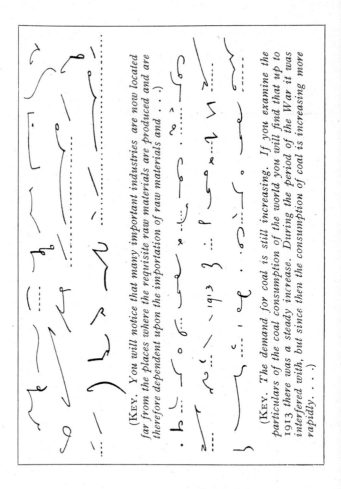

(KEY. You will notice that many important industries are now located far from the places where the requisite raw materials are produced and are therefore dependent upon the importation of raw materials and . .)

(KEY. The demand for coal is still increasing. If you examine the particulars of the coal consumption of the world you will find that up to 1913 there was a steady increase. During the period of the War it was interfered with, but since then the consumption of coal is increasing more rapidly. . . .)

(KEY. I have been informed that this meeting is duly constituted in accordance with the Statutes to transact all the business which is to be brought before it. I presume it is your pleasure that the report and accounts circulated among you be taken as read. Before I give you an account of the conditions under which your establishment has worked during the past year I have the pleasure to report to you the signature of new agreements . . . .)

A point that is naturally frequently raised in the discussion of high speed is: "What is the most desirable size of shorthand characters to be adopted?" On this question it is impossible to be dogmatic, as here again individuality asserts itself. The natural tendency of some writers is to write in a "dainty" style, with the notes somewhat packed, others write the characters small, but allow more space between the outlines, while others adopt a freer and larger style, with possibly more suggestion of "dash" in it. That each and all of these methods can be effective has been amply proved from personal experience of the work of advanced writers. A recent examination of the speed notes of six 200-words-a-minute writers shows that the number of outlines contained in a line of a Pitman's Fono Notebook, No. 20 ($4\frac{3}{8}$ in.), varied from eight to twenty. It will be seen, therefore, that the disparity is rather a wide one, and in view of the fact that the writers concerned have all proved their high speed ability over and over again it is obvious that the "ideal" size cannot be fixed within narrow limits.

Objection may be taken to the very small and crowded notes because of the eye-strain involved in transcribing: there is also the difficulty of securing absolute accuracy of detail.

Probably twelve to fourteen outlines to a line would be found to be a good average. A little experiment in this direction should be interesting, although we would warn students not to allow the desire to write a certain number of outlines to a line to become an obsession, or to interfere in any way with accurate note-taking.

In the cases mentioned it is noteworthy that the students who are "finger writers," that is to say, those who write with very little hand movement but manipulate the pen chiefly through the movement of the thumb and the first two fingers, are inclined to write very small notes. When the movement of hand and arm is more obvious the tendency is to take more space for writing.

Should it be found that there are less than ten outlines on an average to the line, it is worth while to pause and consider whether it might not be more advantageous to conserve space and possibly energy by employing a slightly smaller and more compact style of outline formation. It is needless waste of energy, for instance, to persist in a four-outlines-to-a-line style, possibly dwindling to two in the right-hand bottom corner of the page—a style which is by no means unknown in shorthand classes and which teachers very rightly discourage. This style is entirely devoid of advantage. It has, in fact, distinct disadvantages, not the least of which is the very frequent necessity for turning over the pages. Anyone who has a tendency to write in this way should make every effort to counteract it. A good remedy is to have an abundance of practice at a speed well below one's capabilities, and to make a point of writing full lines always.

In this connection there is another point that is worthy of consideration. If one watches an expert speed typist at work, one is immediately impressed by the precision and rapidity with which the carriage is returned. Not a fraction of time is wasted. In the same way the shorthand writer must cultivate similar quickness of movement in the return of the hand from the end of one line to the beginning of the next. The reader is recommended to practise this "return" until he is able to assure himself that it could not be done more quickly. Probably he will find his left-hand margin somewhat irregular at first, but gradually he will acquire the ability to "land" on the right spot with unfailing accuracy. In this movement the hand should not leave the paper: it should simply *glide* to the starting point. This is not an unimportant detail.

While slow practice is in progress the writer must not relax and fall into the error of forming the outlines in a careless or slovenly way: a real endeavour must be made all the time to improve outline formation. This point is emphasized because observation has shown that many students, capable of writing, say, a hundred words a minute, when asked to take down a passage at sixty words a minute immediately fall into the error of relaxing, and assume a careless attitude, the head comfortably propped on the left hand being a particularly favoured position.

"Speed is valueless unless it be accompanied by the ability to produce legible notes. It may not be possible to write at the rate of 180 or 200 words a minute with that degree of precision and correctness that may characterize notes written at half that speed, but it is possible, as has been demonstrated by high speed writers on numerous occasions, to write phonography at the rate of over 200 words a minute in such a manner that the notes can be read with ease. If from the commencement of his practice the student makes a determined effort to form the phonographic characters as perfectly as the circumstances allow, he will find that as he increases his dexterity with the pen there will be little loss of legibility."—
The late Phil. P. Jackson, Certificated Writer of Pitman's Shorthand at 210 words a minute.

CHAPTER SEVEN

MANUAL DEXTERITY

To anyone who is interested in the art of short-hand—and, indeed, to many who have no practical knowledge of the subject—there is something akin to fascination in watching outline after outline flash in effortless manner from the pen of the expert as it glides across the page of the notebook. This dexterous pen manipulation constitutes, per-haps, one of the most noticeable differences be-tween the tyro and the advanced speed writer. The former will probably find that in the early days of his speed training his progress across the page will not be as the swallow, but will bear a closer resemblance to that of the frog—a series of "jumps," with a pause between each jump. To eliminate this jerkiness in his writing, and to cultivate a smooth, gliding movement, is a task to which he should earnestly devote himself, as spasmodic movement is a very real hindrance to speed. In some measure it is due to inexperience and possibly anxiety, but is largely the result of an insufficiency of practice on the right lines.

To acquire skill in this direction admittedly entails the exercise of a certain amount of patience and concentration, but the student with ambition and with intelligent perception will be only too willing to make what little effort is called for. It is to be feared that very many students do not realize to the full extent the great part which manual dexterity plays in speed writing. They are aware, possibly, that slowness and awkwardness of hand movement are among their weak points, and realize that they are definite handicaps to progress; but, apart from taking dictation in the ordinary way at home or in class, they take no active steps to cultivate greater facility in writing. Actually this is a side of the training which is of paramount importance. The student who desires to join the ranks of the high speed writers must not overlook the fact that, though the practice and advice he receives in class are bound to have beneficial results, no art which calls for speed in mind or body can be brought to its fullest perfection by the teacher's efforts alone. *The student must help himself, seriously and conscientiously.*

Pianists, violinists, dancers, high speed typewriter operators, and others who are desirous of reaching the highest state of efficiency, must give many hours of conscious effort to acquiring and retaining the necessary skill and flexibility which makes for that "effortless" execution which is characteristic of the expert. So, also, in the field of sport: the cricketer who, with a lightning turn

of the wrist, sends the bowler's fastest ball career-
ing to the boundary, or the footballer who, with
twinkling feet, outwits his opponents with apparent ease, has given time and study to the deliberate
cultivation of that dexterity which makes his
display outstanding.

The shorthand writer must train with equal
diligence if he wishes to excel in his art, and in
this chapter a few suggestions are made by means
of which he can help himself to eliminate awkwardness or hesitancy in outline formation.

Holding the Pen.

The manner of holding the pen is one of the
first considerations, and is most certainly deserv-
ing of some thought and experiment. It is not
sufficient merely to take up the pen "anyhow"—
there is a right and a wrong way for each individual. Slow progress in speed is very often
traceable to a faulty method of holding the pen
left uncorrected. The learner who finds the
formation of outlines somewhat awkward, and
lacking in that facility which is so essential for
speed, should, by experiment, find out if there
is not some other way of holding the pen that
would bring about the desired improvement. It
is more than likely that he will. It may be that
the fingers are too near or too far away from the
point of the pen; that the thumb is too far

forward, or that the hand is lying too flat and heavily on the paper. Whatever the cause, it is clear that it must be remedied, and the method most suited to the individual should be sought for and cultivated until it becomes quite natural.

If progress in speed is slow and unsatisfactory, therefore, this matter of holding the pen should not be overlooked when possible causes are being considered. The pen should be held in a manner that allows such forms as

to be written smoothly, lightly, and quickly.

Our observation has shown that the majority of high speed writers of our acquaintance favour a short grip. On the following pages we reproduce two photographs illustrating one method of holding the pen which has proved highly satisfactory. In this case the writer favours, after experiment, what some may consider an exceptionally low grip. A little point to note is that the thumb and the forefinger touch lightly.

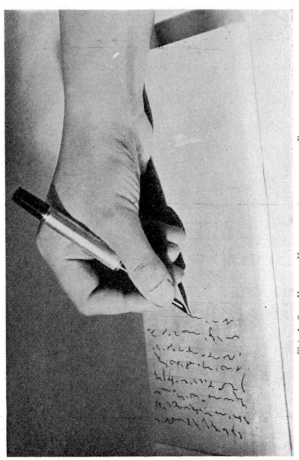

Plate 1—Side View of Hand, showing position of Fingers

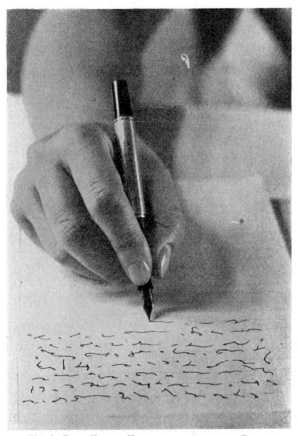

Plate 2—FRONT VIEW OF HAND, SHOWING POSITION OF FINGERS

It is not suggested, of course, that this is the only correct way of holding the pen. As we have said, there is a right and a wrong way for the individual writer, and he must experiment until he is satisfied that he has found a method which gives him satisfactory control over the pen.

As a general rule, the forefinger should lie on top of the barrel of the pen, with the second finger inclined to be below the barrel, and the remaining fingers "folded" comfortably under-neath in such a manner that the whole hand rests lightly on the outer edge of the small finger. (The writer's weight should rest on the left fore-arm in order to give the fullest freedom of move-ment to the right hand.) The thumb should act as assistant to the first finger, and should rest only lightly against the pen. Lightness of grip is a very important factor. Many students, in the early stages particularly, favour a vice-like grip. So far, we have not heard of a fountain pen snapping under the pressure, but should such a thing hap-pen in a shorthand class it would not occasion us undue surprise! This tendency is quite a natural one, especially when writing at or near the limit of one's speed. Actually, however, it is very detrimental so far as speed is concerned, as it restricts the full movement of the pen and puts considerable strain on the arm muscles, which very quickly results in that tired feeling in the arm of which so many are the victims, even after only a five-minute spell of writing. It is essential, therefore, that the student during his practice should always be on the alert to counteract this inclination. In time a light, but nevertheless firm, grip will become natural.

One other point which should here be stressed is that the wrist should never rest flat on the notebook or desk, as this definitely prevents free, easy movement across the page. In the majority of cases it will be found most suitable if the points of contact on the notebook and the desk respectively are the edge of the small finger and the middle of the forearm. In other words, there should be a little "daylight" showing beneath the wrist.

Incidentally we recommend the writer not to transfer the cap to the top of the pen for note-taking. Except in the case of a very short pen, a better balance is obtained if the cap is removed altogether.

Touch.

Allied with the suggested light grip there should, of course, be a light style of writing. The motorist does not travel along the highway with his brakes applied—neither should the shorthand writer expect to achieve a good speed across the page of his notebook if he is writing "with the brakes on," which, in a measure, is what happens when the pressure of the pen on the paper is unnecessarily heavy. Every effort should be made to develop a light touch, and regular practice will quickly show a great improvement. Admittedly, some very capable speed writers press rather heavily on the paper, but in the case of the majority of writers a light style is much more likely to produce the best results in the matter of speed. The light strokes should be *hair* strokes, with only the slightest extra pressure for the heavy strokes.

Apart from the speed value of this style of writing, it has, as we have said, the additional virtue of being more pleasing to the eye, a fact which can make work much more pleasurable.

The student may not find his writing comes up to his ideal—how many things do?—but so long as he can experience inward pleasure from the work he has accomplished his progress is bound to be steady. Pride begets enthusiasm, and enthusiasm occupies an important position in the "progress department" of any walk in life.

Facility.

Dexterity and accuracy of pen movement being outstanding essentials of the speed writer, it naturally follows that a goodly proportion of the time devoted to practice should be occupied in seeking to reach the highest state of excellence

72

possible in this respect. In fast writing there must be absolute control over the pen. As a matter of fact, the degree of control possessed by the writer represents to a considerable extent the difference between the expert and the moderate writer. If the aspiring student has an opportunity of observing an expert writer at work or practice, he should note the ease and speed with which outlines are transferred to the paper. Outlines which the learner would probably write in sections, as it were, flash from the expert's pen without any appreciable pause at any point. The acquirement of this enviable dexterity should be begun very early in shorthand training. There is, in fact, no reason why it should not begin with the first lesson.

Many shorthand students fail to realize that, if they but make the effort to acquire pen control, there are quite a number of forms which they could write as quickly as the fastest writer in the world. Such outlines as ╱ ╲ are cases in point. Perhaps at first there may be a slight but distinct pause between the ╷ and the ╱, or the ╷╷ and the ╲ ; but, by practice, it will be found that the outlines can be completed almost as soon as the pen touches the paper.

When the speed of writing such simple forms as these is greatly accelerated attention should be given to somewhat longer forms. A little experiment with such forms as ⌒ ⌒ will soon show that they can be written at very high speeds, although the tyro may find that at first he retains the same pressure on the pen throughout these and other outlines—that he "draws" them, even although he draws them quickly. The accomplished writer, on the other hand, immediately he turns the hook of the *f* in *refer*, simply "flicks" the *ray*, letting the end of the stroke, as it were, look after itself. Strictly, the pen begins to leave the paper before the end of the stroke is reached. In the same way, the ⌒ in *require* can be flicked with no noticeable pause after the *ray*, and the outline written at an amazing speed. This ability to flick strokes has a great influence on speed. To illustrate the point we give below several outlines written in the first line as by a slow and inexperienced writer, and in the second as by a more accomplished writer.

In the first set of outlines there is a lack of "swing," and it will be seen, particularly in the last three outlines, that pressure on the pen has been maintained until the end of the outline, whereas in the second specimen there is obvious evidence that the final strokes have been flicked. The tapering of the *b* in *n-b* should be noted. This tapering is indicative of the fact that the pressure on the pen has been relieved actually before the end of the stroke is reached, and this is a quality which writers will do well to cultivate. The learner should also bear in mind that such joined strokes as *f-downward r, qu-downward r,* and *n-m* should be visualized and written as *one* form, not as two separate strokes. They should be written in a smooth, flowing style, with no break at the junction of the two strokes. This point has a most important bearing on speed writing.

To furnish material for practice of the kind under discussion, two notebooks have been prepared: *Facility Notebook for Speed Students* and *Phrase Drill Notebook*. In the *Facility Notebook* there is a series of graded word and sentence exercises, in shorthand, covering all the rules of the system. This book can be used by both elementary and advanced students. The " drills " consist of five lines of shorthand, each followed by three blank lines. The student should first read the lines of printed shorthand and then copy the outlines on the first blank line, writing neatly and carefully, and mentally repeating the words as they are written. This mental repetition of the words is recommended as a guard against the writing being done mechanically, with little or no mental activity.

It is preferable to work *across* the page, writing each outline once only. The second and third blank lines should then be similarly filled in, an effort being made at each repetition to increase the speed of writing. When the page has been completed in this way the student should start at the top again, and repeat the process. This writing may be done over the first, as in the example here given—

The exercises in the *Facility Notebook* are so arranged that the book may be used from the beginning of the study.

The *Phrase Drill Notebook* is on similar lines, and contains a series of graded exercises ranging from elementary phrasing to the most advanced. Those who work through this book in the manner suggested will therefore acquire a sound know-ledge of the art of phrasing as well as the ability to write over nine hundred frequently-occurring phrases with ease and swiftness, an accomplishment which obviously must have a great and beneficial influence on the speed of the writer.

In this type of practice it is absolutely essential that the student's powers of concentration be exerted to the utmost, and a real effort made to form the outlines neatly, lightly, and quickly. The pen should never be removed more than a fraction of an inch from the surface of the paper, and the passage from one outline to the next should be as smooth as possible; that is, there should be no *jumping* from one to the other. Nor should the writer "ease up" when a line has been completed. The hand should, as we have said, flash back to the starting point on the next line in the fraction of a second. This quick return, when cultivated, will prove of the greatest value in high speed work, in which seconds and fractions of seconds often mean the difference between success and failure. There should be nothing casual about this practice. The hand-on-the-head attitude—which posture at once reveals the student lacking the vital spark of enthusiasm—is of little or no value.

It is a good plan to time oneself when engaged in this practice. For instance, one might set the standard of, say, ten minutes to copy out one page of the *Drill Book* neatly, and to go over the outlines three more times, which would mean writing sixty lines of shorthand in ten minutes. As skill increases this time limit could, of course, be reduced. Some writers are able to complete a page four times in five minutes. The facility and powers of concentration developed through this practice are bound to have an effect on subsequent note-taking.

Both these books, by the way, contain the letterpress *keys* for reference.

Further suggested drills will be found in *Facility Exercises for Shorthand Students*.

This form of practice can, of course, be extended. In the course of speed practice, for instance, there are sometimes outlines which cause momentary hesitation and consequently slight loss of speed, due to lack of complete knowledge of the correct forms. It is suggested that students should have a small notebook in which to record the outlines for such words, and any others that may be dealt with during the lesson. The outlines for the words *threshold, wholeheartedly, fertilizer, Mediterranean, obsolescence, inconsistently, disastrous,* for instance, which have occurred in recent test papers, might give some inexperienced writers pause, and such outlines should form the basis of further drills for spare moments, until the writer is so familiar with them that they flow from the pen as easily as would the outlines for the simplest of words.

It is our opinion that the writing of a series of varied outlines is much more beneficial than the writing of a single outline many times, as the monotony of writing one form over and over again tends to make the writer careless of accurate formation.

Another variation of this form of practice is to copy a piece of connected matter, say, a past examination paper, leaving blank lines for practice. Such a passage should be written several times in the manner already described, until it can be completed neatly and fluently at a speed thirty or forty words a minute above the examination rate.

Periodic practice of this nature is definitely helpful, and is strongly recommended, particularly to those students entering for examinations. It ensures an increase of facility, and if, as suggested, past examination papers are chosen, it gives, in addition, a clear idea of the type of matter favoured by the examiners.

Students should give at least ten minutes a day to such facility exercises. Even where a student's time is fairly well occupied, there are very few who cannot at some time of the day afford to give this amount of time to practice in manual dexterity.

For odd moments there are many exercises for "finger loosening" and pen control, and, as a matter of interest, we reproduce a section from a speed writer's notebook illustrating a few of such exercises.

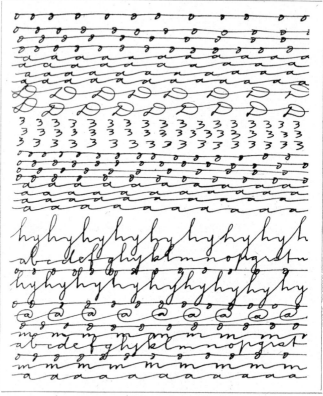

It may not be found easy at a first attempt to write a complete line of, say, joined o's or a's, but after a little practice greater pen control will be acquired. As with the other exercises, these should be done with enthusiasm and concentration, and a definite attempt to increase the speed should be made. Any exercise which calls for rapidity of finger and hand movement and pen control must assist the writer towards high speed, and, as will be obvious, there is ample scope for the student to enlarge upon the number of such exercises.

As figures frequently occur in both business correspondence and examination tests it is well that the student should be able to write the figures *one* to *nine* rapidly and unmistakably, and for this reason we recommend that he should seek to acquire facility in this respect. Some of us are inclined to put in unnecessary little flourishes when writing figures. All suggestion of flourish should be eliminated when forming figures in the course of dictation, and the shorthand writer should, therefore, practise writing the figures rapidly and with the greatest economy of line. The following style is simple and clear—

1234567890

Apart from the method of representing figures explained in the *Shorthand Instructor*, there is an interesting section on this aspect of the subject in *Technical Reporting*, by Thomas Allen Reed, from which excellent book the following extracts are taken—

There are certain contractions in connection with figures which may be used with advantage and the author recommends the following, which he has for years employed in his own practice.

The common fractions $\frac{1}{4}$, $\frac{1}{2}$, $\frac{3}{4}$, which, if they occur frequently, are much too long for the writer, may be thus abbreviated—

$\frac{1}{2}$ by a straight stroke above the figure to which it belongs, as $\overline{2} = 2\frac{1}{2}$, $\overline{5} = 5\frac{1}{2}$.

$\frac{1}{4}$ by a straight stroke in the same position, with an *initial* tick or hook, as $\overline{} = 1\frac{1}{4}$, $\overline{2} = 2\frac{1}{4}$.

$\frac{3}{4}$ by a straight stroke in the same position, with a *final* tick or hook, as $\overline{4'} = 4\frac{3}{4}$, $\overline{16'} = 16\frac{3}{4}$.

$\frac{3}{4}$ when occurring by itself may be written ꝛ ; and $\frac{2}{3}$ may be written ᶾ .

Hundreds may be written with a straight horizontal stroke by the side of the figure to which it belongs, thus $4— = 400$; $16— = 1,600$.

Thousands may be written with a straight horizontal or slightly sloping stroke under the figure to which it belongs, thus $7\diagup = 7,000$; $120\diagup = 120,000$; $3\diagup = 300,000$; $5\diagup = 500,000$.

Pounds (whether in money or weight, the context distinguishing), may be expressed by a dot following the figure to which it belongs, thus—

1. = £1 or 1 lb.

5. = £5 or 5 lb.

4— = £400 or 400 lb.

10 = £10,000 or 10,000 lb.

3 = £300,000 or 300,000 lb.

If the writer, following very closely upon a speaker, writes the stroke to represent thousands and finds that other figures follow, he can write them under the stroke, instead of erasing it, as—

5240 = 5,240; 361 = 3,061; 89 = 8,009.

If these practical methods of figure representation appeal to the speed student he should practise them until he is able to use them in his notes with ease and accuracy.

All the suggestions so far made for the acquirement of dexterity of penmanship have the advantage that they call for purely personal expenditure of time and effort, and may be indulged in at any time, although, of course, it will be obvious that such forms of practice could be adopted by the teacher in the speed class. As a matter of fact, a great many successful teachers find these and similar exercises an interesting and beneficial diversion from the straightforward dictation which must necessarily occupy the major part of the lesson.

Apart from such drills as have been indicated, repetition practice, with its many variations, is a well-known and widely adopted method of speeding up the pen. In this respect, however, the teacher must exercise his discretion in the matter of the rate of speed dictated and the length of the test.

If the students are keen and enthusiastic, they will naturally be desirous at times of attempting speeds which are really beyond their present capabilities; but the benefit to, say, a 120 words a minute writer of endeavouring to record a passage at 150/160 words a minute, if of long duration, is somewhat problematical, as such attempts usually result in mental chaos and several pages of a notebook filled with ill-formed outlines, many of which defy transcription. Such experiences are more apt to demoralize than to encourage students. Nevertheless, all teachers realize that the really eager student is a prize, and his enthusiasm should be fostered in every possible way; and the *successful* taking down of a passage considerably beyond one's usual speed *is* an incentive to further effort. We suggest, therefore, that higher speeds should sometimes be dictated, but that it is preferable in the majority of cases to confine the attempt to short passages only. If, for example, the practice is to be at 20 words a minute over the student's reliable speed the matter could be dictated in half-minute spells, as it is generally within the ability of a writer to sustain a somewhat higher speed for this short time, with a fair measure of success.

A suitable passage having been selected the first half-minute should be dictated, followed after an interval not exceeding fifteen seconds by the second half-minute. After a further very brief interval the whole minute should be dictated. If there has been any doubt about the correct outlines for any of the words or phrases opportunity should be taken by the student at this point to ascertain the authorized forms. The second minute of the passage should then be dealt with in exactly the same way, after which the two minutes should be dictated without a break. The slight familiarity with the matter will lessen the mental strain, and the writer should be able either to take it successfully or at any rate to get within measurable distance of it. The matter might be dictated several times until it can be written neatly and with a *swing*.

If, as a matter of interest, a rate higher than twenty words a minute over the normal speed is attempted, it is suggested that the passage be dealt with along similar lines, but in quarter-minute spells. In this case, each quarter-minute might be read twice before proceeding to the next quarter.

A further variation of this "speeding-up" practice is to dictate the matter very rapidly, not in half or quarter minutes, but in single sentences (or part of the sentence if it is too long), allowing time at the end of each sentence for the students to complete their note of it. Here, again, it is advisable to dictate each sentence more than once before proceeding to the next.

The teacher will, of course, be able to adapt this type of practice in many ways according to the needs of his class.

For instance, he might dictate for one minute at 80 words a minute, read the same passage at 100 words a minute (with the necessary extra words), and so on until he has reached the limit of the ability of the class. (100-words-a-minute students would probably be able to reach 160 words a minute on this.) Or he might read a five-minute passage at 80 words a minute, and re-read it at 100 and then at 120 words a minute. Alternatively, the teacher could choose a test at a speed approaching the limit of the student's ability, and dictate it a number of times at the same speed.

The value of repetition practice at the same rate of speed lies chiefly in the fact that it affords the students an opportunity to improve their style of writing at high speed, and this is a point that the teacher should emphasize at all times.

Dictation at rising speeds is another method which inculcates the spirit of keenness. Where, for example, the average rate of speed in the class is about 120 words a minute, the passage should be marked off in minutes at 100, 110, 120, 130, and 140 words a minute. Teachers will find that students almost invariably show an enthusiastic interest in striving to record the passage while the speed is being gradually accelerated.

In leaving this side of the training of the speed student, we reiterate that in all these varied forms of practice, as in the ordinary work of the class, there must be nothing lackadaisical in the student's attitude. There should be close concentration and unrelaxing effort throughout.

Tackled in the right spirit repetition practice can be of the greatest assistance, for the hand and the brain are in this way gradually trained to work harmoniously together at higher speeds. It has been argued that repetition practice tends to make the writing mechanical, or at any rate careless, but if the student is consciously making a genuine effort to write neatly and with accuracy, that alleged objection is dispelled. The cultivation of rapid movement in the formation of outlines for a wide variety of words is bound to have a beneficial effect on the speed writing abilities of the students. The opinion occasionally expressed that repetition work gives students a false idea of their speed capabilities is rather a reflection on the commonsense of the students. The arguments against the employment of this method seem to us to be outweighed by the undoubted benefits derived from its judicious use, and in our opinion it has a definite place in the training of the speed writer.

CHAPTER EIGHT

MENTAL ALERTNESS AND CONCENTRATION

In shorthand writing the writer must always, of necessity, be some words behind the speaker. It follows, therefore, that while he is writing one set of words he has to listen to, and hold until the appropriate moment, another set. This is impossible unless the mind and the hand are working in complete unison. We have already spoken of manual dexterity and now come to the vital necessity for mental alertness.

Some people assert that this cannot be cultivated. While this may be true in certain isolated cases there can be little doubt that it *can* be cultivated. Mental alertness and the ability to concentrate are not the prerogative of the few. Take as a homely example the case of the present-day pedestrian, whose lot in this motoring age "is not a happy one." Can it be denied that within the last ten years the average pedestrian has cultivated additional nimbleness of eye, brain, and foot? If he had not, the race would by now probably be extinct!

Just as the pedestrian has, of necessity, learned

to get across the street quickly, so must the shorthand writer train himself to get across the page quickly. Obviously, one *must* be wide-awake mentally to write shorthand *quickly*.

We are fortunate in the fact that it is unnecessary to go outside our own particular subject to find one of the best means of developing mental alertness, for there is nothing more likely to develop that quality than the exercise of the hand and brain in the effort to take down the words of a really fast speaker. Even though in the training period we fail, as we sometimes will, the very act of concentrating all our faculties in a genuine attempt to record the words heard must have a beneficial effect in stirring up a mind which may be inclined to be sluggish.

There must, however, be real concentration. What we may call semi-concentration, when even at a fairly high speed the mind will wander to other subjects quite apart from the work in hand, is not in our opinion of much assistance in so far as cultivating mental alertness is concerned. This brings us to a point in the training at which a great many promising writers fall by the wayside. They do not make the progress they might make simply and solely because they lack, or rather have not developed to its full extent, this power of concentration. They may *think* they concentrate, but how many actually do? It would be an interesting experiment for a shorthand teacher, after dictating a passage, to ask the members of his class how many of them had, during the notetaking, thought of nothing but the writing on which they were engaged. If they were candid the majority of them would have to admit that their thoughts had wandered considerably.

It may not be possible to banish every extraneous thought from the mind while taking down, even at very high speeds, but with the majority of students closer concentration is undoubtedly possible. The mind must, for the time being, be concerned absolutely and exclusively with the work in hand. There must be no "wool-gathering."

As we have said, the writer can do a great deal himself to improve his powers of concentration by fully exercising those powers during actual notetaking. There are, however, various other methods which have been found interesting and beneficial in the shorthand class and which can, of course, be adapted by students for practice outside the classroom.

The teacher might occasionally read to the class comparatively short passages on a variety of subjects, first reminding the students of the necessity for concentration on the sense of the matter and afterwards asking individual students to give him briefly the gist of each passage taken down. Commercial letters are particularly suited to this form of exercise.

Another exercise is for the teacher to dictate a passage well within the ability of his students, after announcing that he does not wish them to begin until a certain word, which he mentions, has been reached. The word in question should be about ten or twelve from the beginning. The students' object is to listen carefully to the opening words, and, immediately the specified word is reached, to begin to write and try to catch up with the reader. This form of practice not only develops powers of concentration but also trains students to remain calm in the midst of a flow of words. The passage need not be a long one—only a few sentences—but the practice should be done regularly.

If, during practice, the speed of dictation happens to be well below the writer's reliable speed, he should occasionally allow himself deliberately to fall behind in this way, and then try, as before, to get level with the reader. This ability—the ability to "sprint" when occasion arises—has an undoubted value, and the short-hand writer who is conscious of possessing this power can tackle his real work with the confident knowledge that should he, through circumstances, fall behind he will have no difficulty in recovering the lost ground.

An excellent exercise for the training of the retentive faculties is for the teacher to ask the students to listen with close concentration to the reading of a sentence or clause of some 15/20 words in length and, after the reading, to write the sentence in shorthand as accurately as they can remember it. It will be found that with a little practice, and in a very short time, they will be able to cope with a considerably increased number of words. In some cases students can remember correctly as many as 30/35 words in this way. This word-carrying ability is generally found to be more marked in the higher speed writers, and there can be little question that it is one of the shorthand writer's greatest assets. It is, therefore, well worth while for the teacher to encourage the slower students to cultivate this ability, and much can be done by the simple method suggested. The practice makes an interesting diversion in the speed class, and has the virtue that students are generally keenly interested in it, there being the slight element of competition.

A variation of this method is the reading of short sentences, say of about ten words, as fast as the words can be uttered, the students being encouraged to exhibit equal celerity in recording the words. This is a real brain stimulator.

Success in high speed depends, naturally, to a

large extent on the ability of the writer to cope with a rapid flow of words, and the inexperienced listener will often find himself unable to "hear" or comprehend matter read at 200 words a minute, even though there is no question of reproducing it in shorthand. Matter read at high speed which may be absolutely intelligible to an expert writer is to him a mere jumble of words. Indeed, members of an audience who have witnessed a demonstration of high speed writing in Pitman's Shorthand have sometimes openly commented on the fact that to them the matter read at the higher speeds was incomprehensible, not through indistinct reading, but on account of the speed.

It is plain, therefore, that the training of the speed writer involves also the training of the ear and the brain to receive matter read at rapid rates. For this reason we suggest that the teacher should occasionally read for a minute at a really high speed, 200 words a minute at least (taking care to articulate quite distinctly), and that the students should be asked not to write but to listen carefully and to try to repeat the matter silently word for word as it is read, keeping within five or six words of the dictator. If this form of exercise is done seriously it is most certainly beneficial from a high speed writing point of view.

It has been said that those who can *read*

shorthand quickly are potential high speed writers, and there is little doubt of the truth of the statement. We have already mentioned the value of shorthand reading as an aid to the acquirement of a good vocabulary; but it has a further value if a point is made of reading the shorthand aloud very rapidly—at 200 words a minute or more. This may seem to a 100-words-a-minute writer a rather high rate, but it is surprising how the reading can be speeded up by practice. The student should select a shorthand passage from, say, *Pitman's Office Training*, and read aloud for one minute, afterwards counting the number of words that he has succeeded in reading. At first it may be found that the speed falls considerably below 200 words a minute, but if the same passage is read a second and a third time a substantial increase in the speed of reading will be apparent. With regular practice of this nature it will soon be possible for him to read from fresh matter at the suggested speed. It is obvious that ability to read at this rate demands concentration and alertness of mind, and for this reason we confidently recommend the speed aspirant to include such fast reading as part of his training.

Dullness or boredom should not be allowed in the speed classroom, and the straightforward dictation matter should be as varied and interesting as possible, as there is no doubt that where interest flags progress will be unsatisfactory. A certain proportion of the pieces dictated should, of course, have a commercial bias, as the majority of students taking up the study are already engaged in, or hoping to take up, office work. But, in view of the tendency of examining bodies to include literary matter in their tests, the general matter should cover an extensive field.

Occasionally as a diversion the teacher might read a commercial letter, not in the manner of the expert dictator, but in the irregular manner, with numerous corrections and hesitations, which is not uncommon in office work. Afterwards the students should be asked to transcribe the matter with the additions and alterations correctly rendered, as if for an employer. This form of dictation may cause a little mild amusement, but it has nevertheless a quite serious value in that, if a correct transcript is to be made, the notetaking must be done with care and alertness.

Shorthand teachers are agreed that there would be many more successes in the shorthand world if students as a whole were less lackadaisical. The lackadaisical student may be seen in almost any classroom—sitting, perhaps, with head resting lazily on the left hand, or sitting well back in the desk and taking a long-distance view of the notebook, far too comfortable, far too leisurely, and possibly writing on a page which is not flat but which bumps up and down as each stroke is written in what would, to a conscientious writer, be a most disturbing fashion! Students have even been observed to yawn in the midst of dictation—a performance which most certainly indicates that they are by no means concentrating. Others seem merely to tolerate the interruption which the taking of notes causes in their surreptitious conversations with neighbours, and barely allow the last word to be dictated before they recommence these interminable confidences. If such "students" are incapable of appreciating the folly of thus wasting their time, the teacher should take an early opportunity of disabusing their minds in no uncertain manner.

High speed will never be attained by leisurely methods, and our advice to students is: if you want to attain high speed, really concentrate; don't be satisfied with half-hearted practice. Half an hour of conscientious effort is worth a week of casual, careless work.

CHAPTER NINE

TRANSCRIPTION

WE have written of the importance of a sound knowledge of the theory, method of holding the pen, manual dexterity, concentration, and other qualities which go towards the making of the expert shorthand writer; but when all is said and done the final proof of ability lies in the transcript, and this side of the training must be treated as seriously as it deserves. Skill in the art of transcription is the ultimate test of the shorthand writer.

Many students, particularly in the early stages, are inclined to look upon transcribing as something in the nature of drudgery, and, unless the teacher has power to insist on transcripts being regularly submitted, will content themselves with "reading through" their notes. (Some will not even do that—yet they expect the teacher to make practical, wage-earning shorthand writers of them.) Although this reading may be checked, and admitting that it is not without considerable value in familiarizing the students with their own particular style of shorthand penmanship, it is not a wholly satisfactory substitute for actual transcription. In reading, mistakes may pass unnoticed, and may, in all probability, be repeated in subsequent work. Weaknesses in spelling and punctuation may remain unrevealed, to appear, perhaps, on some future and more important occasion. Further, when the reading back is done in class it very frequently occurs that when a badly formed outline causes a halt, even though but a momentary one, there is an enthusiast present who will audibly supply the word—well-meant assistance, of course, but assistance which nevertheless deprives the reading of its fullest value.

If the reading of the notes is done privately, there is the obvious temptation to pass by outlines which do not give up their meanings easily. We do not wish to suggest that "reading back" is of comparatively little benefit to a student. It has, as we have said, an undoubted value. Our point is that it should not be wholly accepted as a substitute for actual transcription. Where a class meets for, say, two hours it is perhaps too much to expect that all the matter dictated should be transcribed, as the time that can be given to shorthand outside class must, in most cases, necessarily be confined within certain limits. Where it is at all practicable, however, a pro-portion of the notes taken should be transcribed. Sometimes this transcription could be of the whole of one or two passages, and on other occasions of

short extracts from several of the dictated pieces—
not always from the first minute, of course, where
the strain of prolonged writing has not yet become
apparent. Where the speed is near to the student's
limit of ability there is sometimes a falling-off in
the quality of the notes in the later stages, and it
is well to practise the reading of notes that have
become just a little "wild."

Students who intend sitting for shorthand examinations should note the time taken in such
transcription work. It is a disappointing experience for a student who has succeeded in making
a good note of an examination test piece to find
that, owing to overlooking the time element in
the examination, he is unable to finish his trans-
script. The length of time allowed for transcribing
by examining bodies varies; and part of this
time, it should be emphasized, must be allotted
to the checking of the transcript with the notes.
This checking, by the way, must be carried out
methodically, line by line with the shorthand, as,
in the excitement of the occasion, a word, a
phrase, or even a whole line, may have eluded the
eye. Many of the seemingly inexplicable failures
in an examination could probably be traced to
this cause, as it is by no means uncommon.

Students should, therefore, not be satisfied until
they can transcribe accurately from their shorthand notes at a speed of at least twenty words a

minute. There is, of course, no difficulty in writing at this speed, but in order to maintain such a speed in combination with the reading of the notes students must, naturally, be very familiar with their shorthand notes, and in this respect, as in so many others, it is practice that leads to perfection.

Many of the weaknesses which are to be observed in transcripts are due simply to lack of familiarity on the part of students with their own notes. In support of this we quote the following from the report of the Examiner to the Royal Society of Arts: "Very many sets of shorthand notes were well-written and ought to have been easily deciphered, but a considerable number of the candidates evidently did not devote as much time as they should have done to 'reading back' their own notes or to reading printed or lithographed shorthand matter."

Unfortunately it is not always easy for the teacher to convince certain types of student, especially in evening schools, of the undoubted value of practice in transcribing. The reason given for slackness in this respect is usually "No time." An innocent and gullible teacher might be justified in coming to the conclusion that shorthand students are among the busiest people in the world, with a spare half hour an almost unheard-of luxury! The speed aspirant must not deceive himself into thinking that he has no time for the exercise of his transcribing abilities. He might, with advantage, consider what other busy people have accomplished. He would find that it is generally the busiest people who can find time to do a little more. These "so busy" students appear to look upon practice in the transcription of notes as something to be avoided at all costs. This attitude is utterly wrong, and where it is persisted in satisfactory progress will not be made. If the notes taken at speed are neat and legible, not only will the difficulties of transcription be reduced, but there will be real pleasure in the production of a perfect or well-nigh perfect transcript. Some readers may smile at the suggestion that there is pleasure in transcribing, but let them produce notes that bear the hall-mark of artistic proficiency and, especially in the examination room, that pleasure will be theirs.

Much can be learned from a corrected transcript, provided that the student has the common sense to make a careful study of the errors into which he has fallen. Students should remember that a teacher does not mark a transcript for amusement. A considerable amount of time and trouble is involved in such correction work, and it is done with the sole object of helping the student by pointing out to him where and how he has gone wrong. If the transcript is merely put aside or deposited in the waste-paper basket at the earliest possible moment the student does not derive the slightest benefit from the labour which has been expended on his behalf.

If the transcript is studied, however, very often instances of carelessness, perhaps of stupidity, and sometimes of unsuspected weaknesses in the notes, will be brought to light, while other errors will be traceable to lack of knowledge. In this connection we call to mind an actual case in which an applicant for a position in a solicitor's office was asked, as a test, to take down and transcribe a short letter, in which occurred the sentence: "In the circumstances we are willing to waive the clause." When the letter was typed it was found that this phrase had been rendered: "In the circumstances we are willing to wave the claws."! This mistake was due, obviously, to sheer ignorance of words.

On the other hand, the student who transcribed a sentence, quite well written in shorthand, as "These goods are urgently indeed," instead of: "These goods are urgently needed," presents a splendid example of transcription without applied intelligence. As transcribed the sentence was simply nonsensical, and no one who was following the sense of the passage would have been guilty of such a stupid error. And that brings us to a vitally important word of advice regarding transcription work: transcribe *sense*. That may seem to many to be superfluous advice—and, indeed, it ought to be—but experienced shorthand teachers, and not a few employers, well know how necessary it is.

A disturbing factor, and one which is unfortunately all too common among young students, is the complacency which they exhibit when stupid errors are pointed out to them. They do not seem to realize that when the stern reality of earning a living has to be faced an employer expects, and has a right to expect, a hundred per cent accuracy in the transcript of what he has dictated. In this work-a-day world it is more than unlikely that he will bring back a letter or document, and with a friendly beam say: "You have made only twenty-two errors in this. That's not at all bad." No, his remarks would probably be of a more devastating character!

The aim of the student should be *hundred per cent accuracy*, and he should feel dissatisfied with transcripts that fall below that standard, especially if he is bound to confess to *avoidable* errors. Before shorthand examinations students frequently display an active curiosity in regard to the percentage of error allowed by the examining body. It is very undesirable that a student before an examination or other test of his shorthand ability should thus more or less admit to himself his own incompetency, or subconsciously suggest to himself that he expects to make errors, and that the possibility of his recording a "pass" depends on the number of mistakes allowed by the examiner. His attitude ought, instead, to be one of confidence in his ability to do what he is seeking to do in an accurate and satisfactory manner, and it is only by careful attention to his training that he will develop this belief in himself, a belief which will be of the greatest value to him. Confidence imparts a wondrous inspiration to its possessor, and does much to quell those examination "nerves."

Admittedly, the 100 per cent accuracy standard is one which, even with skill and care, cannot always be maintained. Humanity and the liability to err will ever be associated, and the shorthand writer will now and then be guilty of the Homerian "nod." Apart from such "accidental" errors, transcripts often contain errors and omissions which ought to have been avoided, and the writer must "tackle" his transcript in the way most likely to obviate errors of this kind.

While it is agreed that the ideal is for the shorthand writer to be able to read his notes months or even years afterwards (as, of course, thousands of expert Pitman writers can), we are definitely of opinion that, in the student stage, where an effort is being made to reach this state of perfection, the notes taken at an examination or other test should be carefully read through before transcription. The matter is then still fresh in the mind, and this fact will greatly assist in the deciphering of any outlines which may, through stress of speed, have been badly formed, and which might, in the absence of the precaution of immediately reading through the notes, cause undue delay in the transcript. This initial reading will be rendered much easier if he has acted on the advice already given, and followed the sense of the passage during dictation.

If an outline cannot be read on the preliminary perusal of the notes it should be temporarily passed over, and the reading of the sentence completed. The context will often give a clue to the word required to make the sentence complete. A little experimenting with the vowels should be resorted to if the word still remains elusive. The possibility of an *initial* vowel should not be overlooked.

Another point to be borne in mind is that it is unwise to alter, or add to, the notes in order to "fit in" a word which the faulty outline might be thought to represent. Such a course almost certainly leads to additional errors. In other words: TRUST YOUR NOTES.

Where an outline defies all attempts to decipher

it, it is better frankly to admit inability to transcribe and to leave a blank than to resort to foolish guesswork and produce a group of words devoid of meaning. We have already referred to the necessity for at any rate transcribing *sense*, and a completed transcript, after being checked with the notes, should be read through, time permitting, to make certain that it does make sense. The student, for instance, who, at a public examination, transcribed: "I had read in the works of foreign facilities" instead of: "I had read in the works of various philosophers," and the others who rendered "dry-as-dust Free Traders" as "proud first boast Free Traders" and "try his just Free Traders," had not exercised even the proverbial grain of common sense. Such errors are attributable to nothing but lack of thought, allied with a lamentable weakness in general knowledge. These causes are, as a matter of fact, usually at the root of much of what can only be described as the nonsense that is submitted in transcripts. The remedy for the first defect is obvious, whilst the strengthening of one's general knowledge depends in large measure on intelligent reading and the full exercise of the powers of attention and observation. A healthy curiosity is a valuable asset to the shorthand writer. "All knowledge," said Dr. Johnson, "is of itself of some value. There is nothing so minute, or inconsiderable, that I would not rather know it than not." These words are peculiarly appropriate to the shorthand writer. It has been said with a considerable amount of truth that the shorthand writer should know something about everything. While it may not be possible for him to acquire such an encyclopaedic store of facts, he should lose no opportunities of adding to his knowledge of things in general. He should keep in touch with what the world is doing by reading a responsible newspaper, and, say, one or more of the weekly or monthly literary periodicals. The knowledge thus gained of the world of men and books is a useful social asset, apart from its value from a purely shorthand writing point of view.

The reporting of lectures, addresses, etc., which can be attempted when a reliable speed of about 120 words a minute has been attained, is a great aid, not only in increasing speed, but in broadening one's general knowledge. It is not suggested, of course, that a speed of around 120 words a minute is sufficient for reporting work: it will be inadequate in many cases, but the practice will be helpful. Where the speed is too high for a complete note the writer should aim at getting complete sentences rather than disjointed parts of sentences.

Broadcast talks and speeches are admirably suitable for practice of this kind, and for the embryo reporter it has the advantage that his attempts at speech recording can be done in comparative privacy. Some writers of modest speed might find it somewhat embarrassing to make the attempt "full in the public eye," especially if the speed were beyond their present powers. One of the writers of this book has a vivid and uncomfortable recollection of a first attempt at reporting, with a speed of 130 words a minute. The scene was a village hall, and the youthful reporter occupied a very prominent position near the front, in full view of the best part of the audience. The speaker, a lady, started off, and for at least two lines of the note-book the scribe was "with her." Too late was made the discovery that the lady was a human tornado, speaking at well over two hundred words a minute. To give in openly was too much for youthful pride, and, no doubt to the amazement and admiration of those around, the pencil of the "speed merchant" kept dashing across the page for a full half-hour. The note at the end of the lady's address consisted of a word or two of hers occasionally, interspersed with "Now is the time for all good men to come to the aid of the party," "The boy stood on the burning deck," "What are the wild waves saying?" and such-like sentences. Fortunately, no one asked for a transcript! Needless to say, subsequent attempts at reporting were made from less conspicuous positions.

The wireless is perhaps the best medium for the writer still on the lower rungs of the speed ladder, although some of the talks are delivered at a speed which can hardly be described as slow. In such cases the writer should make an endeavour, as we have suggested, to record as many complete sentences as possible.

Punctuation plays an extremely important part in the production of the accurate transcript, and no shorthand writer can consider himself efficient unless he is conversant with the main rules of punctuation. It is not practicable to insert the punctuation marks, apart from the full stop, *which should never be omitted,* in the shorthand note. Among the most common errors in transcripts is the running of one sentence into another, and the beginning of a new sentence at the wrong place. This is almost invariably due to the omission of the full stop sign in the notes. For instance, if in the shorthand note there appeared the following: "*You will be glad to know that we have continued to make satisfactory progress during the year trading conditions have been difficult but we have managed to weather the storm successfully.*" should it be transcribed: "*You will be glad to know that we have continued to make satisfactory progress. During the year trading conditions have been difficult, etc."* or : *" You will be glad to know that we have continued to make satisfactory progress during the year. Trading conditions have been difficult, etc."*? Reasoning will not help one to the correct rendering in such a case, and from experience we can say that there are many such cases. Therefore, the temptation to omit the full stop during notetaking should be most rigorously resisted. In most shorthand examinations marks are deducted for errors in punctuation, while a business document or report can be completely spoiled by faulty punctuation.

The following brief rules regarding the main points of punctuation, extracted from Pitman's *Punctuation Chart,* will be of interest and assistance—

. FULL STOP is used (*a*) at the close of a sentence; as, *The goods were forwarded by L.M.S. Ry. to-day.*

(*b*) After Abbreviations; as, *G. Astley, Esq., B.A.,* 84 *Cheapside, London, E.C.*2.

: COLON is used before a remark which is of the nature of an afterthought; as, *Invoices to be sent direct to customers : copies to me.*

:— COLON AND DASH are used before a quotation or a list of things; as, *Referring to your inquiry we have a letter from our agent this morning in which he says :—"I have made inquiries about the gentleman to whom you refer and find that he is most highly esteemed."*

;   Semicolon is used when two or more sentences are combined; as, *I called there to-day; saw the manager; and secured the order which is enclosed herewith.*

,   Comma is used (*a*) when it is necessary to indicate a short pause, in order that the sense of the passage may be quite clear; as, *Upon receipt of your cable of the 10th inst., I called upon Messrs. Deakin, who practically control the market at present, and asked them to alter their quotation.*

     (*b*) When it is desired to separate a parenthetical clause from the remainder of the sentence; as, *If this trial order gives satisfaction, as we have no doubt it will, a profitable business may result.*

     (*c*) Before and after words the insertion of which slightly affects the smoothness of a sentence; as, *Kindly examine the account, and, if correct, be good enough to send us a cheque for the amount at once.*

     (*d*) Between two phrases joined by the word "and"; as, *We should be pleased to have your orders again, and we feel sure you would be satisfied with the quality of the goods we are now offering.*

—   Dash is used to mark an abrupt break in the sentence, or it may take the place of brackets; as, *Referring to the consignment of Trimmings—which, by the way, we are expecting daily—we have got in touch with several likely buyers, and we hope to obtain fair prices.*

? NOTE OF INTERROGATION is used (a) after a direct question; as, *May we send you a small parcel at this price?*

The interrogation point is not necessary when the question is only reported to have been asked; as, *I saw the traffic manager, and he asked me when we could supply the necessary details.*

(b) At the end of a sentence which is meant as a query; as, *We presume you would have no difficulty in completing the work by that date?*

' APOSTROPHE is used (a) to mark the possessive case of nouns; as, *We have forwarded to-day, per L.M.S. Ry., a case containing 6 doz. Men's Caps; 4 doz. Boys' Vests; and 3 doz. Girls' Tam o' Shanters.*

(b) To indicate that some letter or letters have been omitted; as, *I don't think it's possible to do anything.*

(c) To indicate the plural of single letters or figures used as words; as, *He must mind his p's and q's.*

" " QUOTATION MARKS are used (a) when the exact words of another person are quoted; as, *Please note that our bill of £250 10s. 6d., due on the 2nd inst., has been returned to us marked " Refer to Drawer."*

(b) When the titles of books, etc., are quoted; as, *I asked his authority for the statement, and he told me he had seen it in " Pitman's Commercial Law."*

Note, however, that a quotation within a quotation is indicated by single marks only; as, *Mr. Walker said, " I charged him with trying to deceive us, and he answered, ' I am not.' "*

In concluding this chapter we would urge shorthand students to give thought to the neatness, as well as to the accuracy, of the transcript. It should not be done hastily, with a wealth of abbreviation and other evidence of lack of pride in the work. In business it is even more desirable that the transcripts, in the form of letters, documents, etc., should be without blemish, correctly punctuated, and set out with due regard for appearance.

CHAPTER TEN

KNOWLEDGE OF WORDS

" It has been said that one of the secrets of high-speed writing is a good general education, and this is true in so far as a command of words is part of a good general education."—R. W. HOLLAND, O.B.E., M.A., M.Sc., LL.D., in *" Principles of Teaching Applied to Pitman's Shorthand."*

UNDOUBTEDLY, one of the essentials in the equipment of the capable shorthand writer, and one of which teachers are always reminding students, is a sound knowledge of current words. Although this is merely stating the obvious, there are, unfortunately, many students who fail to realize the importance of this knowledge, and take no definite steps to add to their limited—sometimes very limited—vocabularies. Bitter complaint has been made by Examiners to the Public Examining Bodies that in a lamentably large number of cases candidates' ignorance of their mother tongue is profound, and accounts for many a failure. Comment is also made that a large proportion of candidates seem to have little or no acquaintance with even the most elementary grammatical rules that govern the use of our language. One of the most widespread complaints made by shorthand teachers regarding their students is that they lack the essential foundation of a sound knowledge of English. And yet, in spite of the fact that students cannot be unaware of their failings in this respect, the English class, in evening institutes at any rate, is the one that is most consistently "dodged" by students taking a course— a very short-sighted policy. Students who have an opportunity of attending such classes should by all means avail themselves of it. Where attendance at a class is not possible, one of the many interesting textbooks on the subject should be studied.

It may be platitudinous, but it is nevertheless an indisputable truth, that when the work of transcription has to be undertaken one's knowledge of words and their usage has an important bearing upon the degree of accuracy of the transcript.

There can be no doubt that a "word sense"— the possession of knowledge that renders it possible to appreciate the *type* of word that would be employed in certain circumstances—is an advantage to the shorthand writer. Even outlines which have been badly formed under the stress of speed will usually yield their secret to the writer whose knowledge of words is sufficient to enable him to realize at any rate what *type* of word or words is essential to make the passage "read sense."

Words, as we are often reminded, are the shorthand writer's stock-in-trade, and it seems strange that many students display a deplorable weakness in this regard, a weakness to which teachers and examiners and employers frequently give sorrowful testimony.

We have mentioned badly formed outlines as being responsible for hesitation in transcribing, but, on the other hand, an examination of students' notebooks will often reveal the fact that outlines which were represented by blanks in the transcript were, as a matter of fact, quite legible, a clear indication that the words had been heard distinctly and that the speed was not abnormal. Such omissions are more often than not simply the result of an insufficient knowledge of words, or the manner in which they are employed.

Sometimes in notetaking the occurrence of an unfamiliar word results in a blank in the note itself and possibly in a faulty rendering of several other words as the direct consequence of the momentary upset. Such words may quite often have been met in the course of reading but carelessly or indifferently passed by. Or, again, it may be that the writer is not altogether unacquainted with the word. He may have seen it on many occasions in newspaper or book, and may, up to a point, appreciate its meaning, but he has not taken the trouble to confirm his mental pronunciation of the word with that of the dictionary. As a result he may hear the correct pronunciation for the first time from the dictator, and may not, therefore, immediately recognize it. This, as likely as not, will have an unsettling effect, and may easily cause the loss of a word or two if the speed of dictation is fairly rapid. Such words as *formidable, desultory, subaltern, amicable, nonchalantly, vagaries, controversy, inventory,* may be cited as examples of the type of word in question. It is surprising how widespread is the mispronunciation of these and other words. May we suggest that the reader, as an interesting little experiment, compares his mental pronunciation of these words with the dictionary pronunciation, noting particularly the accented syllables.

Students sometimes explain omissions in transcripts by stating that they "did not hear" the words. While readers of shorthand tests cannot, of course, claim infallibility in the matter of enunciation, it is to be feared that in a great many cases the gaps could more accurately be attributed to ignorance or, at best, a half knowledge of the word or words "not heard." Examples of this, taken from a Shorthand Examiner's Report, are the very common expressions *Imperial Preference* and *synthetic dyes* rendered as *ethereal preference* and *St. Ethics dyes*. The word *ethereal* was, moreover, spelt, in a great many cases, with an *i* instead of the *e*.

The student who finds himself handicapped by

such lack of knowledge should, in his own interests, do all he can to strengthen this vulnerable point. The words which have caused delay, or have had to be left untranscribed, must not be allowed to escape, as there is always the possibility that they will re-appear on another and perhaps more important occasion, and cause similar trouble. Where practicable they should be traced and their meanings and outlines mastered. All of us have our hobbies, and collecting has countless adherents. The things collected are of extraordinary variety, and some of them, viewed from the standpoint of the disinterested outsider, appear to be singularly purposeless. From out the miscellaneous assortment of hobbies the shorthand writer can pick one that is both pleasurable and profitable, namely, *word-collecting*. We agree that as a hobby it fails in one respect—the word-collector cannot experience the joy his fellow-collectors extract from exhibiting their collections to admiring visitors. His reward lies chiefly in the consciousness that, as time goes on and his collection grows, the danger of being "stumped" by a word becomes less and less, and his efficiency as a writer naturally increases correspondingly. It is hardly necessary to add that, leaving shorthand out of the reckoning, the ability to understand and employ a wide range of words has a definitely cultural value. Word-collecting can be as fascinating as any other form of collecting, and its interest for the collector tends to increase rather than to decrease with experience. Furthermore, it can be indulged in at any time.

The question naturally arises as to how a good vocabulary may be built up. Primarily, an extensive knowledge of words is the result of intelligent reading and observation, for, useful as it is to acquire familiarity with lists of words, a word does not really *live* until it takes its rightful place in phrase or sentence. If, in the course of reading or conversation, a word is used which strikes an unfamiliar note, the student must not be satisfied to let it pass. To ignore a new word is a lapse of which the shorthand writer should never be guilty. Some form of note ought to be made, written if possible, and a reliable dictionary referred to for the meaning and pronunciation. We say "written if possible" because we realize that in certain circumstances a mental note must suffice. One might perhaps be looked at askance if, during a conversation, one produced a notebook and pencil, and made frequent and surreptitious notes! This would be carrying our collecting to undue lengths. Nor should the subject-matter of the conversations of our friends and acquaintances be looked upon as mere hunting-grounds for new words and the subject-matter partly or wholly ignored, as embarrassing situations, to say the least, might arise! But, mentally or in writing, new or half-known words—potential stumbling-blocks to the notetaker—should be noted in a book kept specially for the purpose, and their meanings, usage, and pronunciations ascertained.

To be on the look-out in this way for words need not in any way interfere with the enjoyment to be derived from reading—it should, as a matter of fact, heighten the pleasure.

The lists thus collected should be referred to in spare moments in order to gain thorough familiarity—not merely a "nodding acquaintance"—with the words recorded, and the shorthand writer will find that in this way he acquires a vocabulary which will be invaluable to him in his work.

Shorthand writers who are already in employment, and who naturally desire to increase their proficiency in every way, should not overlook the possibilities of their own trade journals in this connection. Almost every business or profession has its own trade paper or house organ, and by intelligent reading of these the writer would not only increase his working vocabulary but at the same time increase his knowledge of the profession in which he is engaged.

The shorthand writer who aspires to reporting work, or who is not content to be proficient in only one department of shorthand writing but wishes to be a shorthand writer in the real sense of the term, capable of taking notes on a wide variety of subjects, should take steps to make himself familiar with the words in everyday use in the various spheres of human activity. His self-training in this direction need not be entirely through the medium of reading in the accepted sense. By looking at placards, posters, notices, shop-windows, and so on, with a "seeing" eye instead of bestowing on them a casual glance, and by really *listening* to the announcements, talks, and news bulletins on the wireless instead of vaguely "hearing" them, quite a surprising increase can be made to one's store of known words.

As an item of more than passing interest to the word-collector, we may mention that in the *New English Dictionary* there are 414,825 words, and of these 177,970 are described as "current," so that the shorthand writer has, beyond all question, a wide field for exploration!

Spelling

While a wide knowledge of words is an essential qualification of the shorthand writer, that knowledge must be supplemented by the ability to spell correctly the words which have to be transcribed. Faulty spelling can mar the work of the shorthand writer, and, in business, cause annoyance even to the most placid of employers. Where that feeling is aroused frequently in the heart of the employer the career of the delinquent will to a large extent be jeopardized.

Our language is admittedly inconsistent, and sometimes very puzzling, in the matter of spelling, even to educated people. In that connection the following newspaper report is interesting—

A clergyman, a lawyer, and two school teachers, engaged in a spelling contest at Lincoln, Nebraska. A fifth friend submitted a list of ten words. The school teachers misspelled six words each, the clergyman eight, and the lawyer eight. The words they were asked to spell were: supersede, rarely, picnicker, kimono, liquefy, battalion, tranquillity, sacrilegious, naphtha, and paraffin.

It is, however, the shorthand writer's duty to rise superior to the vagaries of English orthography. Not all employers are themselves irreproachable in this respect, and, though they may not admit it, they are dependent on the shorthand writer to see that all documents or letters leaving the office over their signatures are without blemish.

Sometimes, of course, though spelling may not be their strong point, they do notice errors, as, for instance, in the case of one who, after reading through a letter, summoned the shorthand writer to the presence, and said: "Look here, in the first paragraph you spell receive *recieve*, and in the third paragraph you spell it *receive*. That won't do. Put it right!" The young lady agreed that it wouldn't do, and asked: "Which one shall I alter, sir?" He hesitated for a moment or two, and then replied: "Well, er—er—alter the one that's wrong, of course!"

It is a commonplace remark that the study of shorthand has a detrimental effect on one's spelling ability, but it is undoubtedly a fallacious statement. Probably it is nearer the truth to say that the act of transcribing serves to expose many unsuspected weaknesses. Where the slightest doubt exists about the correct spelling of a word the dictionary should be called into use: the dictionary, in short, should be the shorthand writer's companion and should always be within easy reach.

Spelling ability is very largely a matter of observation and of visualization, and in the course of general reading the writer should, as already suggested, cultivate an inquisitive eye, and make a mental note of the spelling of the words met with. This undoubtedly demands close concentration, for, as we all know, it is possible to read and understand a passage and yet fail to appreciate with exactitude the arrangement of the letters in certain words. The gardening enthusiast, for example, may read through with keen interest the magnificent catalogue sent forth by the seedsman, but in filling up his order form how often will he have to refer to this catalogue for the spelling of what are to him everyday words, such as *nasturtiums*, *chrysanthemums*, *antirrhinums*, and *rhododendrons*? Actually, although he has seen the words thousands of times, he has failed to *observe* them properly. He has simply accepted the words in their entirety but not in detail, and finds himself, when the need arises, quite unable to visualize them.

In the matter of proper names, too, the shorthand writer must be careful, particularly in correspondence, as many people are strangely jealous of the correct rendering of their patronymic. Mr. Smythe, for instance, might be righteously indignant to find himself addressed as Smith, or Mr. Thomson to see a *p* wedged in the middle of his name. The following extract from that delightful book *Leaves in the Wind*, by A. G. Gardiner, may here be appropriately quoted—

"To misspell a man's name is to imply that he is so obscure and so negligible that you do not know how to address him and that you think so meanly of him that you need not trouble to find out. It is to offer him the subtlest of all insults—especially if he is a Scotsman!"

While some employers are careful to volunteer the correct spelling of a proper name, there are many who fail to do so, and in such cases the correspondent's letter should, if possible, be referred to. Failing this, the necessary inquiry should be made. As far as practicable proper names written in shorthand should be vocalized.

We give below a list of one hundred words which are in common use but which, despite that fact, are very frequently maltreated in the matter of spelling—and pronunciation. For that reason we suggest that the reader should study their spelling carefully and make certain by consulting the dictionary that he knows their correct pronunciations and meanings. Incidentally, he will find it an interesting experiment to test his friends' spelling powers. Even though the words are common it is more than likely that he will be surprised at the number of people who fail to register a hundred per cent accuracy.

Accommodation, adviser, aerate, affect, affiliation, afforestation, allege, allotment, aluminium, Arctic, auspicious, automaton, bankruptcy, benefited, bicycle, calendar, consensus, demarcation, develop, development, disease, dishevelled, dynamic, effect, élite, emaciate, embarkation, embarrass, enervating, etymological, exaggerate, exhilarate, exorbitant, foregather, forego (go in front), forgo (do without), fulfil, gauge, gramophone, harass, indictment, ingenuous, inimical,

innovation, invincible, irresistible, losing, main-
tenance, manoeuvre, mischievous, negotiate, nonchalantly, nucleus, occurred, occurrence, panacea,
parallel, paucity, permeate, phenomenon, phleg-
matic. physiological, precede, preponderance,
principal, principle, prognostication, propaganda,
proprietary, proprietor, psychological, queue,
quinquennial, recuperate, relinquish, repercussion,
resuscitate, rhythm, salient, seize, separate,
skilful, stationary, stationery, steadfast, straitened,
stupefy, supersede, sustenance, taciturn, threshold,
tranquillity, unmistakable, unparalleled, unsaleable, vicious, vicissitude, vouchsafe, woollen, yield.

CHAPTER ELEVEN

SHORTHAND EXAMINATIONS :
A FEW HINTS

EACH year thousands of shorthand writers seek to set the hall-mark of efficiency on their short-hand work by entering for one or more of the shorthand Examinations arranged by the several Examining Bodies throughout the country. Much has been written for and against Examinations, some affirming that, as candidates are often labouring under the handicap of "nerves," they are consequently incapable of giving of their best. While there can be no question that *some* students fail to do themselves complete justice at Examinations, that does not seem to us to be sufficient justification for discounting entirely the value of such Examinations.

A shorthand speed certificate has an undoubted commercial value. Looked at from a purely utilitarian point of view, a letter of application for a situation, supported by the statement that the writer is the holder of a recognized speed certificate, is bound to influence prospective employers in favour of the applicant, and, as a result, an interview is more likely to be granted than if no definite qualifications could be offered. Competition to-day in the commercial sphere is keener than it has ever been, and the certificated writer is in possession of a very strong initial advantage.

Apart from the commercial aspect there is the pleasure—why should we deny it?—to be derived from worthy personal achievement. Speed aspirants should not, therefore, shirk examinations, but welcome them as tests by which they can estimate their advancement.

Students training for a specified examination are more likely to make the most of their time and opportunities than are those who are more or less casual in their attitude towards the subject they are studying. They have an object in view, and they train accordingly, just as an athlete trains for a sporting event.

The decision to enter for an examination should not be belated. It is of little use to drift along, and then, at the last moment, decide to "have a shot at it." If the examination is to have a successful outcome, the preparation should be thorough and painstaking.

Failure in a shorthand examination may be traced, perhaps, to three main causes: poor knowledge of the theory; lack of general knowledge; and insufficient practice in the gentle art of transcribing. These three points have already been dealt with, and it is unnecessary to reiterate what has been said; but we hope that none of our readers will be found guilty on any of these counts, at any rate. If they are sound in these things success is not likely to be denied them.

There are, however, a few further points which deserve consideration, and attention to these will, we think, go far towards ensuring success. We give them below in the form of a few "Do's and Don'ts for Examinees"—

In the first place, don't under-estimate the difficulty of the Examination, and don't over-estimate the allowance made for errors. You will be putting yourself in a false position if you rely on the examiner being "kind."

On the other hand, don't worry too much about the Examination. Have faith in yourself, and remember—this is a very comforting thought—that you have on many previous occasions demonstrated your ability to do what you are attempting to do in the Examination.

Don't under-estimate the length of time for which you will have to write. Tell yourself that the dictation will go on interminably, and don't relax until you have written the last word. If you allow yourself to think: "Surely it must be nearly finished now!" you will probably relax, and, as likely as not, lose some words.

Don't let the thought steal in : "Oh, I'm getting it down!" or the same thing might happen.

Premature congratulation or jubilation is not conducive to concentration.

Try to ignore the committee or invigilators, who must necessarily be present. They are more concerned with the reader, to see that he reads the passage correctly, and that he does not read, say, the 140 test at about 110 words a minute! If one of them happens to be near you, don't imagine that he is watching you and gloating over every wrong outline that you write! He has other things to think about.

When taking the actual notes make a real endeavour to concentrate very closely and to *follow the sense of the passage being read.* Don't look upon it merely as a mass of words strung together.

Vocalize, if possible, any unusual word, especially proper names. Don't represent proper names by writing the initial capital letter only. In one examination a number of students represented the words "Perth to Adelaide" as P. to A. But in the same piece there occurred the words "Paris to Athens," which they represented in the same way, and the result was hopeless confusion.

After the dictation take time, as we have already suggested, to read through the notes before beginning to transcribe. The matter is still fresh in your memory, and the correct interpretation of any badly-formed outlines is more likely to be arrived at then than later. Time spent in this way is well worth while.

Another warning which we might repeat is, if you cannot make sense of one outline don't alter the surrounding words in order to make that one outline fit in—in other words, *trust your notes.*

Although the time factor is important, don't "dash off" a transcript and rush home. The transcript should be checked word for word with the notes. No prize is granted for the first one out of the Examination Room.

When transcribing don't spend too much time puzzling over a doubtful outline. Leave a gap and complete the transcript as far as possible. When that is done go back and try to fill in the gaps. Careful consideration of the context will suggest the type of word which is essential, and enlightenment frequently follows.

Always have a spare pen or pencil handy, and before the Examination see that the pen is full and working well. Playing the chief character in the Tragedy of the Pen That Ran Dry is an unhappy role.

Use a notebook with which you are accustomed, but see that there are plenty of clean pages in it. It is rather unsettling, to say the least, to find on turning over a page that the following one is already full of shorthand notes. This, by the way, is not an unusual occurrence.

Don't think that copious notetaking on the last day or two will atone for months of slackness, or that practice in transcription can be left until the evening of the Examination.

Don't be satisfied with your notetaking until you feel confident of submitting transcripts that are at least 99 per cent accurate.

Do not, in the weeks preceding an Examination, look upon the teacher of a speed class as a mere gramophone, and ignore all he has to say to you and show you between the dictation of passages. He is really trying to help. Some students are inclined to pay not the slightest attention to the various points explained by the teacher. What teacher has not had the exasperating experience of having *more or less* patiently to explain that an outline asked for is already on the board? Many students, we are sure, do not quite realize how exasperating they can be to even the most good-humoured and long-suffering teacher. Chief among the delinquents are the would-be "cacklers," to whom an hour's work, unrelieved by irrelevant chatter, seems to be an ordeal too great to be borne. They talk, if they are allowed, up to the very moment of the start of the dictation, and at the end of the passage they are ready and anxious to resume their interrupted conversation. Those who suffer from this "urge" should try to realize that inopportune talk is unmannerly, unfair to their fellow-students who are seriously desirous of improving their abilities, unfair to the teacher, and unfair to themselves.

Another pre-Examination injunction is, don't despise taking down at a speed lower than what you consider to be your highest. Even if the speed is twenty or thirty words a minute below your speed, take it down, and strive to increase the neatness and accuracy of your notes. This neatness and accuracy is bound to be reflected in notes written at a higher speed, and transcription is thereby made easier. It is, therefore, very desirable steadfastly to cultivate a good style of writing. The more difficult the work and the more trying the circumstances, the more will the value of a good note become apparent.

Throughout this book we have stressed the importance of neat and accurate notes: but in the examination room it is not only the neatness of the shorthand notes that should interest the examinee. In the majority of cases the transcripts have to be written in longhand, and the candidate should make every endeavour, in the time at his disposal, to ensure that his transcript is at least pleasing in appearance. A hastily scribbled and much-altered transcript does not make a favourable impression. It is quite possible to write neatly *and* rapidly, and prospective candidates should see that this ability is among their accomplishments.

Perhaps the greatest secret of the success which is attained by outstanding people in any calling is that they have worked *hard*; they have had a determined purpose, and sturdy adhesion to it in spite of all difficulties has been the fundamental reason for their success. Pachman, the famous pianist, for example, was reputed to have played certain pieces many thousands of times before he would venture to perform them in public. His genius, therefore, had a very solid foundation of hard work behind it. Such intense physical and mental exertion is not necessary to achieve excellence in the writing of Pitman's Shorthand, but in this, as in every art, the measure of our success largely depends upon personal effort.

The Father of Success is Work—
Get acquainted with the Old Man!

Facsimile of Miss Smith's Speed Notes

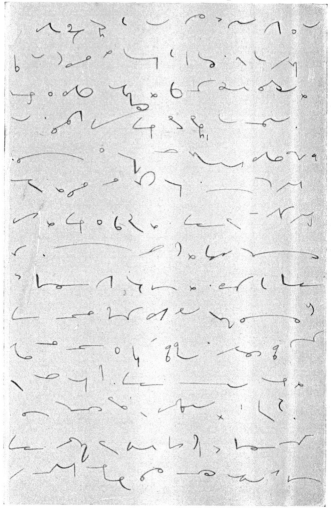

Facsimile of Mr. Munro's Speed Notes

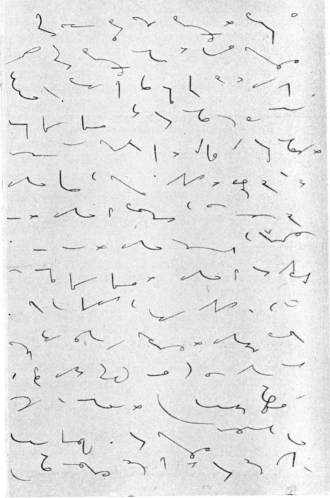

Key to Miss Smith's Speed Notes

We have consistently pointed out that any loss of the lighting load is in itself not so serious as the fact that it affords an opportunity for our competitor to extend his services in other directions. This is actually what is now happening. In a household where electricity has been substituted for gas-lighting the consumer has paid the cost of bringing the service from the street cable to his house and has also bought a meter or rented one. Electricity is thus established. The electrical people quite rightly are not content to let the matter rest there. They want the remainder of the domestic load for that home. Consequently they dangle electric cookers, thermal storage, and so on, before the consumer's eyes, and if his gas cooker is out of date and he is considering a replacement he is likely to be influenced into trying electrical cooking instead. The same argument applies to water-heating. On top of that the electrical refrigeration people who have now turned their attention to the domestic market are carrying out extensive sales campaigns in London and the Home . . .

Key to Mr. Munro's Speed Notes

There have been critical speeches from the supporters of the Government. Everybody has realized, especially the supporters of the Government, in view of the various proposals that they have been putting forward during this two days' Debate as to what we should do to get out of our difficulties, that the Budget in this year is not going to make any appreciable difference to the general conditions which obtain in this country. We have been advised that perhaps a return to the Gold Standard would be all to the good. We have been told over and over again that more economy would be a good thing. We have been reminded that bimetallism

might get us out of our difficulties. We have been told
by the Right Hon. Gentleman, the Member for Darwen,
that if we returned to old-fashioned Free Trade that
would solve our problems. We have heard the Hon.
Member who told us that one of the essential things
was some reform in the machinery of Government. After
having heard all those suggestions, and having taken
into consideration the Budget proposals, I am certain
that even if all those experiments were tried and the
Budget were allowed to . . .

SUPPLEMENTARY CONTRACTIONS

(The following lists contain a selection of alternative outlines given in Pitman's *Shorthand Dictionary*, together with abbreviated forms for a number of miscellaneous words of fairly frequent occurrence. A few of these outlines are unorthodox, and are included as a matter of interest, as they have been found useful in reporting work.)

above-mentioned		banknote	
affidavit		beforehand	
agriculture-al		benevolence-t	
agriculturist		bookshop	
antagonistic		brotherhood	
appreciation		burdensome	
archbishop		cabinet	
aristocracy } aristocratic }		captain	
		casual-ly	
astonish-ed } astonishment }		charabanc	
		clearing-house	
astonishing		cogency	
astonishingly		constitutional-ly	
auspicious		controversy-ial	
auspiciously		counterclaim	
banking		declaration	

defendant		experience-d	
degeneration		extraordinarily	
delinquency		extraordinary	
delinquent		extravagance-t-ly	
democracy		Fahrenheit	
democratic		foundation-stone	
depreciate-d		fugitive	
depreciating		fulfilment	
depreciatory		generation	
derivative		haphazard	
development		headquarters	
dignify-ied		henceforth	
dignity		high-pressure	
dignifying		horticulture-al	
dilapidate-d		immeasurable-ly	
dilapidation		imperialism	
dilapidating		impoverishment	
discrepancy		impregnable-ly	
dissimilar		inauspicious	
divergency		indefatigable	
drunkenness		indescribable-ly	
electrification		indignant	
embankment		indignation	
expectation		indignantly	
expeditiously		indiscriminate	

indiscriminately		philanthropist	
infinitesimal		potential	
irredeemable		practitioner	
journalism		preferential-ly	
journalist		prerogative	
journalistic		preservation	
locomotive		question	
longest		referring	
longitude		regeneration	
machinery		registrar	
man-of-war		remunerative	
melancholy		resignation	
merchantman		ship-builder	
microscopic		solicitor-general	
negotiation		stepping-stone	
neighbourhood		stock-in-trade	
obscurity		strengthening	
observation		stumbling-block	
orthodox-y		superscribe-d	
particularize		suspicious	
permanent		suspiciously	
petroleum		thenceforth	
phenomena		trade-mark	
phenomenon		Transatlantic	
philanthropic philanthropy		transcribe	

transform-ed		urgency	
transformation		vice-chairman	
turnover		workmanship	
unconstitutional-ly		workshop	
under-secretary		Birmingham	
unfortunate		Great Britain	
unfortunately		Johannesburg	
unhesitatingly		Liverpool	
unprecedented		New York	
unprecedentedly		San Francisco	
unrealizable		United States	
unremunerative			

The following books are specially mentioned in this Guide to High Speed Writing

FACILITY NOTEBOOK
FOR SPEED STUDENTS

A Series of Exercises Designed to Cultivate Manual Dexterity in Shorthand Writing.

This notebook contains a series of drills for practice by students who wish to cultivate high speed. The outlines are given at the top of the page, with blank lines for copying. The drills are carefully graded, and are equally suited for use by elementary and advanced students. Key in letterpress is included.

PITMAN'S PHRASE DRILL
NOTEBOOK

Arranged on similar lines to the FACILITY NOTEBOOK FOR SPEED STUDENTS, with a key in letterpress. There are twenty-six drills, arranged according to the various principles, giving a sound idea of phrasing. It is an essential supplementary aid for students aspiring to high speed.

PHONOGRAPHIC PHRASE BOOK

Deals completely with the general principles of phraseography, and contains a list of over 2,400 phrases that are constantly used, together with exercises giving practice in their use.

PITMAN